William Shakespeare's
# King Henry VI: P
*In Plain and Simple English*

# ■BOOKCAPS

**BookCaps™ Study Guides**
www.SwipeSpeare.com

# Table of Contents

## About This Series

The "SwipeSpeare™" series started as a way of telling Shakespeare for the modern reader—being careful to preserve the themes and integrity of the original. Visit our website SwipeSpeare.com to see other books in the series, as well as the interactive, and swipe-able, app!

The series is expanding every month. Visit BookCaps.com to see non-Shakespeare books in this series, and while you are there join the Facebook page, so you are first to know when a new book comes out.

# Characters

KING HENRY the Sixth
DUKE OF GLOUCESTER, uncle to the King, and Protector
DUKE OF BEDFORD, uncle to the King, and Regent of France
THOMAS BEAUFORT, Duke of Exeter, great-uncle to the King
HENRY BEAUFORT, great-uncle to the King, Bishop of Winchester,
  and afterwards Cardinal
JOHN BEAUFORT, Earl, afterwards Duke, of Somerset
RICHARD PLANTAGENET, son of Richard, late Earl of Cambridge,
  afterwards Duke of York
EARL OF WARWICK
EARL OF SALISBURY
EARL OF SUFFOLK
LORD TALBOT, afterwards Earl of Shrewbury
JOHN TALBOT, his son
EDMUND MORTIMER, Earl of March
SIR JOHN FASTOLFE
SIR WILLIAM LUCY
SIR WILLIAM GLANSDALE
SIR THOMAS GARGRAVE
Mayor of London
WOODVILE, Lieutenant of the Tower
VERNON, of the White-Rose or York faction
BASSET, of the Red-Rose or Lancaster faction
A Lawyer, Mortimer's Keepers

CHARLES, Dauphin, and afterwards King, of France
REIGNIER, Duke of Anjou, and titular King of Naples
DUKE OF BURGUNDY
DUKE OF ALENCON
BASTARD OF ORLEANS
Governor of Paris
Master-Gunner of Orleans and his Son
General of the French forces in Bordeaux
A French Sergeant   A Porter
An old Shepherd, father to Joan la Pucelle

MARGARET, daughter to Reignier, afterwards married to

King Henry
COUNTESS OF AUVERGNE
JOAN LA PUCELLE, Commonly called Joan of Arc

Lords, Warders of the Tower, Heralds, Officers, Soldiers,
Messengers, and Attendants

Fiends appearing to La Pucelle

SCENE: Partly in England, and partly in France

# Act I

## SCENE I

Westminster Abbey.

*Dead March. Enter the funeral of King Henry the Fifth, attended on by the Duke of Bedford, Regent of France; the Duke of Gloucester, Protector; the Duke of Exeter, the Earl of Warwick, the Bishop of Winchester, Heralds, &c.*

BEDFORD.
Hung be the heavens with black, yield day to night!
Comets, importing change of times and states,
Brandish your crystal tresses in the sky,
And with them scourge the bad revolting stars
That have consented unto Henry's death!
King Henry the Fifth, too famous to live long!
England ne'er lost a king of so much worth.

*Hang the skies with black, day give way to night!*
*Comets, showing the change of times and nations,*
*stream your crystal tails across the sky,*
*and with them whip the horrid rebellious stars*
*which agreed to let Henry die!*
*King Henry the Fifth, too great for a long life!*
*England never lost such a valuable king.*

GLOUCESTER.
England ne'er had a king until his time.
Virtue he had, deserving to command:
His brandish'd sword did blind men with his beams:

His arms spread wider than a dragon's wings;
His sparkling eyes, replete with wrathful fire,
More dazzled and drove back his enemies
Than mid-day sun fierce bent against their faces.
What should I say? his deeds exceed all speech:

He ne'er lift up his hand but conquered.

*England never had a true king until him.*
*He had goodness, he deserved to lead:*
*when he waved his sword it blinded men with its reflection:*
*his arms spread wider than a dragon's wings;*
*his sparkling eyes, full of angry fire,*
*drove back and dazzled his enemies*
*more than the midday sun shining straight in their faces.*
*What can I say? There are no words to express his great deeds:*
*he never moved without conquering.*

EXETER.
We mourn in black: why mourn we not in blood?

Henry is dead and never shall revive:
Upon a wooden coffin we attend,
And death's dishonourable victory
We with our stately presence glorify,
Like captives bound to a triumphant car.
What! shall we curse the planets of mishap
That plotted thus our glory's overthrow?
Or shall we think the subtle-witted French
Conjurers and sorcerers, that afraid of him
By magic verses have contriv'd his end?

*We mourn by wearing black: why do we not mourn by shedding blood?*
*Henry is dead and will never come back:*
*we are waiting on a wooden coffin,*
*and death's dishonourable victory*
*is being glorified by our stately presence,*
*like prisoners tied to a chariot in a triumph.*
*What! Are we going to think that unlucky stars*
*overthrew the glory of our king?*
*Or do we believe that the cunning French*
*magicians and sorcerers, through fear of him,*
*cast magic spells to bring about his death?*

WINCHESTER.
He was a king bless'd of the King of kings;
Unto the French the dreadful judgment-day
So dreadful will not be as was his sight.
The battles of the Lord of hosts he fought:
The Church's prayers made him so prosperous.

*He was a king blessed by Jesus;*
*the French won't find Judgement Day*
*as terrible as facing him.*
*He fought his battles for God:*
*the prayers of the church ensured his success.*

GLOUCESTER.

The church! where is it? Had not churchmen pray'd,

His thread of life had not so soon decay'd:
None do you like but an effeminate prince,
Whom, like a school-boy, you may over-awe.

*The church! Where are they? If the churchmen hadn't prayed,*
*he would not have died so soon:*
*all you want is a girlish prince,*
*whom you can dominate like a schoolboy.*

WINCHESTER.
Gloucester, whate'er we like, thou art Protector,
And lookest to command the Prince and realm.
Thy wife is proud; she holdeth thee in awe,
More than God or religious churchmen may.

*Gloucester, whatever we want, you are Regent,*
*and you have command over the Prince and the country.*
*Your wife is arrogant; she's the one who dominates you,*
*more than God or religious churchmen can.*

GLOUCESTER.
Name not religion, for thou lov'st the flesh,
And ne'er throughout the year to church thou go'st,
Except it be to pray against thy foes.

*Do not speak of religion, for you love worldly things,*
*and you never go to church at any time of year,*
*except to say prayers against your enemies.*

BEDFORD.
Cease, cease these jars and rest your minds in peace:
Let's to the altar: heralds, wait on us:
Instead of gold, we'll offer up our arms;
Since arms avail not, now that Henry's dead.
Posterity, await for wretched years,
When at their mothers' moist eyes babes shall suck,
Our isle be made a nourish of salt tears,
And none but women left to wail the dead.
Henry the Fifth, thy ghost I invocate:
Prosper this realm, keep it from civil broils,
Combat with adverse planets in the heavens!
A far more glorious star thy soul will make
Than Julius Caesar or bright--

*Stop these arguments and be peaceful:*
*let's go to the altar: heralds, attend us:*
*instead of gold, will make an offering of our weapons,*
*as we have no use for them now, now that Henry is dead.*
*We can expect the future to be wretched,*
*and babies shall drink the tears of their mothers,*
*the island shall feed on salt tears alone,*
*and there will be none but women left to mourn the dead.*
*Henry the Fifth, I summon up your ghost:*
*make this country prosperous, keep it from civil war,*
*fight the influence of the unlucky planets!*
*Your soul will make far more glorious start*
*than Julius Caesar, or bright--*

[Enter a Messenger.]

MESSENGER.
My honourable lords, health to you all!
Sad tidings bring I to you out of France,
Of loss, of slaughter, and discomfiture:
Guienne, Champagne, Rheims, Orleans,
Paris, Guysors, Poictiers, are all quite lost.

*My honourable lords, good health!*
*I bring you sad news from France,*
*of loss, slaughter and frustration:*
*Guienne, Champagne, Reims, Orleans,*
*Paris, Guysors, Poitiers, they have all been lost.*

BEDFORD.
What say'st thou, man, before dead Henry's corse?

Speak softly; or the loss of those great towns
Will make him burst his lead and rise from death.

*What are you saying, man, in front of the body of dead Henry?*
*Speak softly, or the loss of those great towns*
*will make him burst out of his coffin and rise from the dead.*

GLOUCESTER.
Is Paris lost? Is Rouen yielded up?
If Henry were recall'd to life again,
These news would cause him once more yield the ghost.

*Is Paris lost? Has Rouen been surrendered?*
*If Henry were called back to life,*
*this news would make him give up the ghost again.*

EXETER.
How were they lost? What treachery was us'd?

*How were they lost? What treachery was there?*

MESSENGER.
No treachery; but want of men and money.

Amongst the soldiers this is muttered,
That here you maintain several factions,
And whilst a field should be dispatch'd and fought,
You are disputing of your generals:
One would have lingering wars with little cost;
Another would fly swift, but wanteth wings;
A third thinks, without expense at all,
By guileful fair words peace may be obtain'd.
Awake, awake, English nobility!
Let not sloth dim your honours new-begot:
Cropp'd are the flower-de-luces in your arms;
Of England's coat one half is cut away.

EXETER.
Were our tears wanting to this funeral,
These tidings would call forth their flowing tides.

BEDFORD.
Me they concern; Regent I am of France.
Give me my steeled coat.  I'll fight for France.
Away with these disgraceful wailing robes!
Wounds will I lend the French instead of eyes,
To weep their intermissive miseries.

*[Enter to them another Messenger.]*

MESSENGER.
Lords, view these letters full of bad mischance.
France is revolted from the English quite,
Except some petty towns of no import:
The Dauphin Charles is crowned king in Rheims;
The Bastard of Orleans with him is join'd;
Reignier, Duke of Anjou, doth take his part;
The Duke of Alencon flieth to his side.

EXETER.
The Dauphin crowned king! all fly to him!
O, whither shall we fly from this reproach?

GLOUCESTER.
We will not fly, but to our enemies' throats.
Bedford, if thou be slack, I'll fight it out.

BEDFORD.
Gloucester, why doubt'st thou of my forwardness?
An army have I muster'd in my thoughts,
Wherewith already France is overrun.

*[Enter another Messenger.]*

MESSENGER.
My gracious lords, to add to your laments,
Wherewith you now bedew King Henry's hearse,

There was no treachery, there was a lack of men and
money.
The soldiers are saying that
there are several different parties here at court,
and when the battles should be swiftly fought,
you are arguing over details:
one wants long wars with little expense;
another wants to act swiftly, but doesn't have the means;
a third thinks that peace can be got without
any expense, just through using cunning fair words.
Wake up, English noblemen!
Don't let laziness spoil your newly won honours:
the fleur-de-lis have been cropped from your coat of arms;
you have lost half of it.

If this funeral was not making us cry,
this news would start us.

This is my business; I am Regent of France.
Bring me my chainmail. I shall fight for France.
Enough of these disgraceful mourning clothes!
I'll give the French wounds instead of eyes,
through which they will cry for their regular miseries.

Lords, read these letters full of bad news.
France has completely revolted against England,
except for some little towns of no importance:
the Dauphin Charles has been crowned King at Rheims;
the Bastard of Orleans has joined with him;
Reignier, Duke of Anjou, is on his side;
the Duke of Alencon is hastening to join him.

The Dauphin crowned as King! Everyone rushes to him!
Oh, how shall we escape the shame of this?

We will not flee, except towards our enemies' throats.
Bedford, if you won't agree, I'll do the fighting.

Gloucester, why do you doubt my willingness?
I have already planned how to raise an army,
which in my mind has already conquered France.

My gracious lords, to add to your tears,
with which you now soak King Henry's hearse,

I must inform you of a dismal fight
Betwixt the stout Lord Talbot and the French.

*I must tell you about a terrible fight*
*between the brave Lord Talbot and the French.*

WINCHESTER.
What! wherein Talbot overcame? is't so?

*What! Which Talbot won? Is that it?*

MESSENGER.
O, no; wherein Lord Talbot was o'erthrown:
The circumstance I'll tell you more at large.
The tenth of August last this dreadful lord,
Retiring from the siege of Orleans,
Having full scarce six thousand in his troop,
By three and twenty thousand of the French
Was round encompassed and set upon.
No leisure had he to enrank his men;
He wanted pikes to set before his archers;
Instead whereof sharp stakes pluck'd out of hedges
They pitched in the ground confusedly,
To keep the horsemen off from breaking in.
More than three hours the fight continued;
Where valiant Talbot above human thought
Enacted wonders with his sword and lance:
Hundreds he sent to hell, and none durst stand him;
Here, there, and every where, enrag'd he slew:
The French exclaim'd, the devil was in arms;
All the whole army stood agaz'd on him.
His soldiers spying his undaunted spirit
A Talbot! a Talbot! cried out amain,
And rush'd into the bowels of the battle.
Here had the conquest fully been seal'd up,
If Sir John Fastolfe had not play'd the coward.
He, being in the vaward, plac'd behind
With purpose to relieve and follow them,
Cowardly fled, not having struck one stroke.
Hence grew the general wreck and massacre;
Enclosed were they with their enemies:
A base Walloon, to win the Dauphin's grace,
Thrust Talbot with a spear into the back;
Whom all France with their chief assembled strength
Durst not presume to look once in the face.

*Oh no: in which Lord Talbot was defeated.*
*I'll tell you more about what happened.*
*On the tenth of August, this fearsome Lord*
*was retreating from the siege of Orleans,*
*with hardly six thousand men in his force,*
*and he was encircled and set upon*
*by twenty three thousand French.*
*He had no time to get his men into battle order;*
*he had no pikes to put in front of his archers,*
*and had to make do with sharp stakes cut from the hedges*
*which they stuck irregularly in the ground,*
*to stop the cavalry from breaking through.*
*The fight continued for more than three hours,*
*and brave Talbot did miraculous things with his*
*sword and spear, unimaginable things.*
*He sent hundreds to hell, and nobody could resist him.*
*In his anger he killed those all around him.*
*The French said that the devil had taken up arms,*
*and the whole army watched him astonished.*
*His soldiers, seeing his undaunted spirit,*
*all shouted out, " To Talbot, to Talbot!",*
*And rushed into the heart of the battle.*
*The battle would then have been completely won,*
*if Sir John Fastolfe hadn't been a coward.*
*He was at the back, having been placed there*
*to follow them and provide reinforcements,*
*but he fled like a coward, having not struck a single blow.*
*So the general ruin and slaughter grew.*
*They were surrounded with their enemies.*
*A low villain, to win the approval of the Dauphin,*
*stabbed Talbot in the back with a spear—*
*someone whom all of France, with all their army there,*
*did not dare to look one time in the face.*

BEDFORD.
Is Talbot slain? then I will slay myself,
For living idly here in pomp and ease,
Whilst such a worthy leader, wanting aid,
Unto his dastard foemen is betray'd.

*Has Talbot been killed? Then I will kill myself,*
*as punishment for living the good life here,*
*while such a great leader, lacking assistance,*
*was betrayed to his horrible enemies.*

MESSENGER.
O no, he lives; but is took prisoner,
And Lord Scales with him, and Lord Hungerford:
Most of the rest slaughter'd or took likewise.

*Oh no, he lives; but he is a prisoner,*
*along with Lord Scales, and Lord Hungerford:*
*most of the rest have been killed or otherwise are*
*prisoners like them.*

BEDFORD.
His ransom there is none but I shall pay:
I'll hale the Dauphin headlong from his throne:
His crown shall be the ransom of my friend;

*Nobody but I shall pay the ransom for him:*
*I'll throw the Dauphin headfirst from his throne:*
*his crown shall be the price he pays for my friend;*

Four of their lords I'll change for one of ours.
Farewell, my masters; to my task will I;
Bonfires in France forthwith I am to make
To keep our great Saint George's feast withal:
Ten thousand soldiers with me I will take,
Whose bloody deeds shall make all Europe quake.

MESSENGER.
So you had need; for Orleans is besieg'd;
The English army is grown weak and faint:
The Earl of Salisbury craveth supply,
And hardly keeps his men from mutiny,
Since they, so few, watch such a multitude.

EXETER.
Remember, lords, your oaths to Henry sworn,
Either to quell the Dauphin utterly,
Or bring him in obedience to your yoke.

BEDFORD.
I do remember it, and here take my leave
To go about my preparation.

*[Exit.]*

GLOUCESTER.
I'll to the Tower with all the haste I can,
To view the artillery and munition;
And then I will proclaim young Henry king.

*[Exit.]*

EXETER.
To Eltham will I, where the young King is,
Being ordain'd his special governor;
And for his safety there I'll best devise.
*[Exit.]*

WINCHESTER.
Each hath his place and function to attend:
I am left out; for me nothing remains.
But long I will not be Jack out of office:
The King from Eltham I intend to steal,
And sit at chiefest stern of public weal.

*[Exeunt.]*

*I'll exchange four of their lords for this one of ours.
Farewell, my masters; I'm going to work;
I'm going to light a bonfire in France to
celebrate the feast of our great Saint George:
I shall take ten thousand soldiers with me,
and all of Europe shall quake at their bloody deeds.*

*You will need them; for Orleans is under siege;
the English army has become weak and faint:
the Earl of Salisbury is desperate for supplies,
and can hardly keep his men from mutiny,
since they are so few, and are confronted by so many.*

*Remember, lords, the oaths you swore to Henry,
that you would either completely overthrow the Dauphin,
or make him obedient to us.*

*I do remember, and I'm leaving now
to go and get ready.*

*I'll go to the Tower as quickly as I can,
to inspect the artillery and ammunition;
and then I will declare young Henry as king.*

*I shall go to Eltham, where the young king is,
as I am appointed his special governor;
and there I shall make the best plan possible for his safety.*

*Everyone has his job and duty to do:
I have been left out; there's nothing left for me.
But I won't be left out for long:
I intend to smuggle the king away from Eltham,
and become the one who steers the path of the country.*

## SCENE II.

France. Before Orleans

*[Sound a Flourish. Enter Charles, Alencon, and Reignier, marching with Drum and Soldiers.]*

CHARLES.
Mars his true moving, even as in the heavens
So in the earth, to this day is not known:
Late did he shine upon the English side;
Now we are victors; upon us he smiles.
What towns of any moment but we have?
At pleasure here we lie near Orleans;
Otherwhiles the famish'd English, like pale ghosts,

Faintly besiege us one hour in a month.

*What the god of war really intends, on heaven*
*or on earth, is not clear today:*
*recently he favoured the English side;*
*now we have triumphed; he favours us.*
*What important towns are there that we don't have?*
*We can rest easy here near Orleans,*
*while from time to time the starving English, like pale ghosts,*
*weakly attack us for an hour each month.*

ALENCON.
They want their porridge and their fat bull beeves
Either they must be dieted like mules,
And have their provender tied to their mouths,
Or piteous they will look, like drowned mice.

*They are missing their porridge and their beef:*
*they should be fed like mules,*
*with nosebags over their heads,*
*or they will look pitiful, like drowned mice.*

REIGNIER.
Let's raise the siege:  why live we idly here?
Talbot is taken, whom we wont to fear:
Remaineth none but mad-brain'd Salisbury;
And he may well in fretting spend his gall,
Nor men nor money hath he to make war.

*Let's lift the siege: why are we wasting time here?*
*Talbot, whom we used to fear, has been captured:*
*there's nobody here but the madman Salisbury;*
*and he can waste away his anger in impotent worrying,*
*he doesn't have the men or the money to make war.*

CHARLES.
Sound, sound alarum! we will rush on them.
Now for the honour of the forlorn French!
Him I forgive my death that killeth me
When he sees me go back one foot or flee.

*Sound the charge! We will rush at them.*
*Now for the honour of the desperate French!*
*I forgive anyone for my death if he kills me*
*for going back a single foot or retreating.*

*[Exeunt.]*

*Here alarum; they are beaten back by the English, with great loss. Re-enter Charles, Alencon, and Reignier.*

CHARLES.
Who ever saw the like? what men have I!
Dogs! cowards! dastards!  I would ne'er have fled,
But that they left me 'midst my enemies.

*Whoever saw anything like it? What men I have!*
*Dogs! Cowards! Bastards! I would never have fled,*
*only they left me surrounded by my enemies.*

REIGNIER.
Salisbury is a desperate homicide;
He fighteth as one weary of his life.
The other lords, like lions wanting food,
Do rush upon us as their hungry prey.

*Salisbury is a desperate murderer;*
*he fights like one who doesn't care if he lives.*
*The other lords rush at us as if they were*
*hungry lions who had just seen their prey.*

ALENCON.
Froissart, a countryman of ours, records,
England all Olivers and Rowlands bred
During the time Edward the Third did reign.

*Froissart, one of our countrymen, records*
*that during the reign of Edward the Third*
*only heroic and noble fighters were born in England.*

More truly now may this be verified;
For none but Samsons and Goliases
It sendeth forth to skirmish. One to ten!
Lean raw-bon'd rascals! who would e'er suppose
They had such courage and audacity?

CHARLES.
Let's leave this town; for they are hare-brain'd slaves,
And hunger will enforce them to be more eager:
Of old I know them; rather with their teeth

The walls they'll tear down than forsake the siege.

REIGNIER.
I think by some odd gimmors or device
Their arms are set like clocks, still to strike on;
Else ne'er could they hold out so as they do.

By my consent, we'll even let them alone.

ALENCON.
Be it so.

*[Enter the Bastard of Orleans.]*

BASTARD.
Where's the Prince Dauphin? I have news for him.

CHARLES.
Bastard of Orleans, thrice welcome to us.

BASTARD.
Methinks your looks are sad, your cheer appall'd:
Hath the late overthrow wrought this offence?
Be not dismay'd, for succour is at hand:
A holy maid hither with me I bring,
Which by a vision sent to her from heaven
Ordained is to raise this tedious siege,
And drive the English forth the bounds of France.
The spirit of deep prophecy she hath,
Exceeding the nine sibyls of old Rome:
What's past and what's to come she can descry.
Speak, shall I call her in? Believe my words,
For they are certain and unfallible.

CHARLES.
Go, call her in. *[Exit Bastard.]*
But first, to try her skill,
Reignier, stand thou as Dauphin in my place;
Question her proudly; let thy looks be stern:
By this means shall we sound what skill she hath.

*[Re-enter the Bastard of Orleans, with Joan La Pucelle.]*

REIGNIER.
Fair maid, is 't thou wilt do these wondrous feats?

---

*This can certainly now be seen;
they are only sending out Samsons and Goliaths
into the battle. They were facing odds of ten to one!
Skinny rascals! Who could ever imagine
that they have such courage and nerve?*

*Let's not bother with this town; they are mad slaves,
and hunger will make them even stronger:
I've had experience of them; they would rather tear down the walls
with their teeth than give up the siege.*

*I think there must be some kind of odd machinery
which keeps their arms going by clockwork;
otherwise they could never hold out as they have been doing.
I agree, we won't bother with them.*

*I agree.*

*Where's the Prince Dauphin? I have news for him.*

*Bastard of Orleans, you are triply welcome.*

*I think you look sad, your happiness is gone:
has this recent defeat caused this?
Do not dismayed, help is at hand:
I've brought a holy girl with me,
who has been sent a vision from heaven telling her
that she is the one who will lift this tedious siege,
and drive the English out of France.
She has the gift of farseeing prophecy,
greater than the nine sibyls of ancient Rome:
she can see what's in the past and what's in the future.
Tell me, shall I bring her in? You must believe me,
I'm telling you the absolute truth.*

*Fetch her in.
But first, to test her skill,
Reignier, you pretend to be the Dauphin;
question her proudly; look stern:
this way we'll find out what skills she really has.*

*Fair maid, is it you who can do these remarkable things?*

**PUCELLE.**
Reignier is 't thou that thinkest to beguile me?
Where is the Dauphin? Come, come from behind;
I know thee well, though never seen before.
Be not amazed, there's nothing hid from me.
In private will I talk with thee apart.
Stand back, you lords, and give us leave awhile.

*Reignier, do you think you can trick me?*
*Where is the Dauphin? Come out from hiding;*
*I recognise you, though I've never seen you before.*
*Don't be astonished, there's nothing I can't see.*
*I will talk to you in private and alone.*
*Stand back, you lords, and give us some time.*

**REIGNIER.**
She takes upon her bravely at first dash.

*She carries herself well, from first impressions.*

**PUCELLE.**
Dauphin, I am by birth a shepherd's daughter,
My wit untrain'd in any kind of art.
Heaven and our Lady gracious hath it pleased
To shine on my contemptible estate:
Lo, whilst I waited on my tender lambs
And to sun's parching heat display'd my cheeks,
God's mother deigned to appear to me,
And in a vision full of majesty
Will'd me to leave my base vocation,
And free my country from calamity:
Her aid she promised and assured success:
In complete glory she reveal'd herself;
And, whereas I was black and swart before,
With those clear rays which she infused on me
That beauty am I bless'd with which you may see.
Ask me what question thou canst possible,
And I will answer unpremeditated:
My courage try by combat, if thou dar'st,

And thou shalt find that I exceed my sex.
Resolve on this, thou shalt be fortunate,
If thou receive me for thy warlike mate.

*Dauphin, I was born the daughter of a shepherd,*
*and I have had no sort of education;*
*Heaven and our gracious Lady have been pleased*
*to shed their light on my low position.*
*So, while I tended to my lambs*
*and exposed my cheeks to the burning sun,*
*the mother of God condescended to come to me*
*and in a majestic vision,*
*told me to leave my low occupation*
*and save my country from disaster:*
*she promised her help and that we would definitely win.*
*She revealed herself in all her glory,*
*and, where I was black and swarthy before,*
*she shone her clear rays upon me, to give me*
*the beauty I now have, which you can see.*
*Ask me any question you want*
*and I will answer without thinking;*
*you can test my bravery through single combat, if you dare,*
*and you will find that I am greater than a woman.*
*You must know this: you will be lucky,*
*if you take me on as your partner in war.*

**CHARLES.**
Thou hast astonish'd me with thy high terms;
Only this proof I 'll of thy valour make,
In single combat thou shalt buckle with me,
And if thou vanquishest, thy words are true;
Otherwise I renounce all confidence.

*You have amazed me with your elevated language;*
*I'll just ask for this proof of your bravery,*
*that you take me on in single combat,*
*and if you win, what you say is true;*
*otherwise I won't believe a word.*

**PUCELLE.**
I am prepared:  here is my keen-edg'd sword,
Deck'd with five flower-de-luces on each side,
The which at Touraine, in Saint Katharine's church-yard,
Out of a great deal of old iron I chose forth.

*I am ready: here is my sharp sword,*
*decorated with five fleur-de-lis on each side,*
*which I selected from amongst a great deal of old iron*
*at Touraine, in Saint Katherine's churchyard.*

**CHARLES.**
Then come, o' God's name; I fear no woman.

*Then attack, in the name of God; I'm not afraid of any woman.*

**PUCELLE.**
And while I live, I 'll ne'er fly from a man.

*And while I live, I'll never run from any man.*

*Here they fight, and Joan La Pucelle overcomes.*

CHARLES.
Stay, stay thy hands; thou art an Amazon,
And fightest with the sword of Deborah.

*That's enough; you are an Amazon,*
*and you fight with the sword of Deborah.*

PUCELLE.
Christ's Mother helps me, else I were too weak.

*The mother of Christ helps me, or I could never do this.*

CHARLES.
Whoe'er helps thee, 'tis thou that must help me:
Impatiently I burn with thy desire;
My heart and hands thou hast at once subdued.
Excellent Pucelle, if thy name be so,
Let me thy servant and not sovereign be:
'Tis the French Dauphin sueth to thee thus.

*Whoever is helping you, you must tell me:*
*I am burning with desire for you;*
*you have conquered my heart and my hands at once.*
*Excellent Maid, if that is your name,*
*let me be your servant and not your king:*
*this is the French Dauphin who begs this from you.*

PUCELLE.
I must not yield to any rites of love,
For my profession's sacred from above:
When I have chased all thy foes from hence,
Then will I think upon a recompense.

*I must not give into any sort of love,*
*for I am a servant of those in heaven:*
*when I have driven all your enemies away,*
*then I will think of a reward.*

CHARLES.
Meantime look gracious on thy prostrate thrall.

*In the meantime look favourably on your kneeling*
*worshipper.*

REIGNIER.
My lord, methinks, is very long in talk.

*My lord seems to be talking for very long time.*

ALENCON.
Doubtless he shrives this woman to her smock;
Else ne'er could he so long protract his speech.

*No doubt he's hearing this woman's confession;*
*otherwise he could never speak for so long.*

REIGNIER.
Shall we disturb him, since he keeps no mean?

*Shall we interrupt, since he has no moderation?*

ALENCON.
He may mean more than we poor men do know:
These women are shrewd tempters with their tongues.

*He may be up to more than we poor men can know:*
*these women can be very tempting with their tongues.*

REIGNIER.
My lord, where are you? what devise you on?
Shall we give over Orleans, or no?

*My lord, where are you? What are you planning?*
*Shall we give up on Orleans, or not?*

PUCELLE.
Why, no, I say; distrustful recreants!
Fight till the last gasp; I will be your guard.

*Why, no, I say; faceless cowards!*
*Fight to the last breath; I will protect you.*

CHARLES.
What she says I'll confirm:  we'll fight it out.

*I agree with what she says: we'll fight it out.*

PUCELLE.
Assign'd am I to be the English scourge.
This night the siege assuredly I 'll raise:
Expect Saint Martin's summer, halcyon days,
Since I have entered into these wars.
Glory is like a circle in the water,

*I have been given the task of whipping the English.*
*I shall certainly lift the siege tonight:*
*expect a late Saint Martin's summer, wonderful days,*
*now that I have come into these walls.*
*Glory is like the ripples on the water,*

Which never ceaseth to enlarge itself
Till by broad spreading it disperse to nought.
With Henry's death the English circle ends;
Dispersed are the glories it included.
Now am I like that proud insulting ship
Which Caesar and his fortune bare at once.

CHARLES.
Was Mahomet inspired with a dove?
Thou with an eagle art inspired then.
Helen, the mother of great Constantine,
Nor yet Saint Philip's daughters, were like thee.
Bright star of Venus, fall'n down on the earth,
How may I reverently worship thee enough?

ALENCON.
Leave off delays, and let us raise the siege.

REIGNIER.
Woman, do what thou canst to save our honors;
Drive them from Orleans and be immortalized.

CHARLES.
Presently we 'll try:  come, let's away about it:
No prophet will I trust, if she prove false.

[Exeunt.]

*which never ceases to grow bigger,*
*until it has spread so far it disappears to nothing.*
*With the death of Henry the English ripples end;*
*the glories it encompassed are gone.*
*Now I am like the proud invading ship*
*which carried Caesar and his fate at once.*

*Was Muhammad inspired by a dove?*
*Then you are inspired by an eagle.*
*Neither Helen, the mother of great Constantine,*
*nor the daughters of Saint Philip, were like you.*
*Bright star of Venus, fallen down to earth,*
*how can I worship you enough?*

*No more delay, let us lift the siege.*

*Woman, do what you can to save our honour;*
*drive them out of Orleans and become famous throughout*
*history.*

*We'll try at once: come, let's start:*
*if she is false  I will never trust any prophet.*

## SCENE III.

London. Before the Tower.

*[Enter the Duke of Gloucester, with his Serving-men in blue coats.]*

GLOUCESTER.
I come to survey the Tower this day:
Since Henry's death, I fear, there is conveyance.

Where be these warders that they wait not here?
Open the gates; 'tis Gloucester that calls.

FIRST WARDER.
*[Within]* Who's there that knocks so imperiously?

FIRST SERVING-MAN.
It is the noble Duke of Gloucester.

SECOND WARDER.
*[Within]* Whoe'er he be, you may not be let in.

FIRST SERVING-MAN.
Villains, answer you so the lord protector?

FIRST WARDER.
*[Within]* The Lord protect him! so we answer him:
We do no otherwise than we are will'd.

GLOUCESTER.
Who willed you? or whose will stands but mine?
There's none protector of the realm but I.
Break up the gates, I 'll be your warrantize:
Shall I be flouted thus by dunghill grooms?

*Gloucester's men rush at the Tower Gates, and Woodvile the Lieutenant speaks within.*

WOODVILE.
What noise is this? what traitors have we here?

GLOUCESTER.
Lieutenant, is it you whose voice I hear?
Open the gates; here's Gloucester that would enter.

WOODVILE.
Have patience, noble duke; I may not open;
The Cardinal of Winchester forbids:
From him I have express commandment
That thou nor none of thine shall be let in.

GLOUCESTER.
Faint-hearted Woodvile, prizest him 'fore me?
Arrogant Winchester, that haughty prelate
Whom Henry, our late sovereign, ne'er could brook?
Thou art no friend to God or to the King.

*I have come to take inventory at the Tower today:
I fear that since Henry's death there has been some
pilfering.
Where are those warders who ought to be here?
Open the gates; it's Gloucester giving the orders.*

*Whose that who knocks so arrogantly?*

*It is the noble Duke of Gloucester.*

*Whoever he is, you can't come in.*

*Villains, is this how you answer the lord protector?*

*May the lord protect him! That's the answer we give him:
we're only obeying orders.*

*Whose orders? Who has any power here except me?
I am the only protector of the kingdom.
Open the gates, I shall answer for you:
will I be disobeyed like this by dung shovellers?*

*What's this noise? What traitors are these?*

*Lieutentant, is that you I can hear?
Open the gates; it's Gloucester here, and I want to come
in.*

*Be patient, noble duke; I cannot open the gates;
the Cardinal of Winchester has forbidden it:
I have direct orders from him
that neither you nor any of your men can be let in.*

*Cowardly Woodvile, do you rate him above me?
Arrogant Winchester, that proud churchman
whom Henry, our recent King, could never stand?
You are no friend to God or to the king.*

Open the gates, or I 'll shut thee out shortly.

*Open the gates, or I'll make sure you lose your job.*

SERVING-MEN.
Open the gates unto the lord protector,
Or we 'll burst them open, if that you come not quickly.

*Open the gates to the lord protector,*
*or we'll break them open, if you don't hurry.*

*[Enter to the Protector at the Tower Gates Winchester and his men in tawny coats.]*

WINCHESTER.
How now, ambitious Humphry! what means this?

*Hello there, you ambitious umpire, what's the meaning of this?*

GLOUCESTER.
Peel'd priest, dost thou command me to be shut out?

*You moth-eaten priest, have you ordered me to be shut out?*

WINCHESTER.
I do, thou most usurping proditor,
And not protector, of the king or realm.

*I do, you are a rebellious traitor,*
*not the protector, of the King or the country.*

GLOUCESTER.
Stand back, thou manifest conspirator,
Thou that contrivedst to murder our dead lord;
Thou that givest whores indulgences to sin:
I 'll canvass thee in thy broad cardinal's hat,
If thou proceed in this thy insolence.

*Stand back, you brazen conspirator,*
*you who plan to murder our dead king;*
*you who give whores permission to sin:*
*I'll trap you in your big Cardinal's hat,*
*if you carry on with this insolence.*

WINCHESTER.
Nay, stand thou back; I will not budge a foot:
This be Damascus, be thou cursed Cain,
To slay thy brother Abel, if thou wilt.

*No, stand back; I shall not move an inch:*
*this is Damascus, you can be damned Cain,*
*and kill your brother Abel, if you wish.*

GLOUCESTER.
I will not slay thee, but I 'll drive thee back:
Thy scarlet robes as a child's bearing-cloth
I 'll use to carry thee out of this place.

*I will not kill you, but I'll drive you back:*
*I shall use your scarlet robes like a sling*
*for a child, and carry you out of this place.*

WINCHESTER.
Do what thou darest; I beard thee to thy face.

*Try what you dare; I challenge you to your face.*

GLOUCESTER.
What! am I dared and bearded to my face?
Draw, men, for all this privileged place;
Blue coats to tawny coats. Priest, beware your beard;

*What! You are daring and challenging me to my face?*
*Draw your swords, men, this place has special laws;*
*blue coats against brown coats. Priest, watch out for your beard;*

I mean to tug it and to cuff you soundly:
Under my feet I stamp thy cardinal's hat:
In spite of pope or dignities of church,
Here by the cheeks I 'll drag thee up and down.

*I mean to pull it and give you a good beating:*
*I shall stamp your cardinal's hat under my feet:*
*disregarding the Pope or the dignity of the church,*
*I'll drag you up and down by your cheeks.*

WINCHESTER.
Gloucester, thou wilt answer this before the pope.

*Gloucester, you will answer to the Pope for this.*

GLOUCESTER.
Winchester goose, I cry, a rope! a rope!
Now beat them hence; why do you let them stay?
Thee I 'll chase hence, thou wolf in sheep's array.
Out, tawny coats! out, scarlet hypocrite!

*You old lech, someone bring me a rope!*
*Beat them away; why are they still here?*
*I'll chase you out, you wolf in sheep's clothing.*
*Get out, brown coats! Out, you scarlet hypocrite!*

*Here Gloucester's men beat out the Cardinal's men, and enter in the hurly-burly the Mayor of London and his Officers.*

MAYOR.
Fie, lords! that you, being supreme magistrates,
Thus contumeliously should break the peace!

*Enough, lords! How terrible that you, supreme judges,
should so insolently disturb the peace!*

GLOUCESTER.
Peace, mayor! thou know'st little of my wrongs:
Here's Beaufort, that regards nor God nor king,
Hath here distrain'd the Tower to his use.

*Peace, mayor! You don't know my grievances:
here's Beaufort, who has no regard for God or the King,
who has commandeered the Tower for his own use.*

WINCHESTER.
Here's Gloucester, a foe to citizens,
One that still motions war and never peace,
O'ercharging your free purses with large fines,
That seeks to overthrow religion,
Because he is protector of the realm,
And would have armour here out of the Tower,
To crown himself king and suppress the prince.

*Here's Gloucester, an enemy to citizens,
one who always wants war and never peace,
taking your money out of your purses in levies,
who wants to rule over religion,
because he is protector of the kingdom,
and wants the armour out of the Tower,
so he can crown himself king and depose the prince.*

GLOUCESTER.
I will not answer thee with words, but blows.

*I'll give you your answer with blows, not words.*

*Here they skirmish again.*

MAYOR.
Nought rests for me in this tumultuous strife
But to make open proclamation:
Come, officer; as loud as e'er thou canst.

*There's nothing I can do about this battle
but to make an open announcement:
come, officer; as loud as you can.*

OFFICER.
All manner of men assembled here in arms
this day against God's peace and the king's, we charge
and command you, in his highness' name, to repair to

your several dwelling-places; and not to wear, handle, or
use any sword, weapon, or dagger, henceforward, upon
pain of death.

*All of you men who have gathered here with weapons
today against the peace of God and the King, we order
and command you, in the name of his Highness, to go back to
your residences; and not to wear, handle, or
use any sword, weapon or dagger, from now on,
on pain of death.*

GLOUCESTER.
Cardinal, I 'll be no breaker of the law;
But we shall meet, and break our minds at large.

*Cardinal, I shall not break the law;
but we shall meet and fight with our minds.*

WINCHESTER.
Gloucester, we will meet; to thy cost, be sure;
Thy heart-blood I will have for this day's work.

*Gloucester, we will meet; you can be sure you will lose;
I will have your blood for what you've done today.*

MAYOR.
I 'll call for clubs, if you will not away.
This Cardinal's more haughty than the devil.

*I'll tell my men to use their weapons, if you won't go.
This cardinal is more arrogant than the devil.*

GLOUCESTER.
Mayor, farewell: thou dost but what thou mayst.

*Mayor, farewell: you're only doing what you have to.*

WINCHESTER.
Abominable Gloucester, guard thy head;
For I intend to have it ere long.

*Disgusting Gloucester, watch your head;*
*for I intend to have it off before long.*

*[Exeunt, severally, Gloucester and Winchester with their Serving-men.]*

MAYOR.
See the coast clear'd, and then we will depart.
Good God, these nobles should such stomachs bear!
I myself fight not once in forty year.

*See that the coast is clear, and then we will leave.*
*Good God, the way these nobles carry on!*
*I myself have not fought a single time in forty years.*

*[Exeunt.]*

## SCENE IV. Orleans.

*[Enter, on the walls, a Master Gunner and his Boy.]*

MASTER GUNNER.
Sirrah, thou know'st how Orleans is besieged,
And how the English have the suburbs won.

*Sir, you know how Orleans is under siege,*
*and how the English have captured the suburbs.*

BOY.
Father, I know; and oft have shot at them,
Howe'er unfortunate I miss'd my aim.

*I know that, father; I have often shot at them,*
*but unfortunately I've always missed.*

MASTER GUNNER.
But now thou shalt not. Be thou ruled by me:
Chief master-gunner am I of this town;
Something I must do to procure me grace.
The prince's espials have informed me
How the English, in the suburbs close intrench'd ,
Wont through a secret grate of iron bars
In yonder tower to overpeer the city,
And thence discover how with most advantage
They may vex us with shot or with assault.
To intercept this inconvenience,
A piece of ordnance 'gainst it I have placed;
And even these three days have I watch'd,
If I could see them.
Now do thou watch, for I can stay no longer.
If thou spy'st any, run and bring me word;
And thou shalt find me at the governor's.

*But you won't now. Do as I say:*
*I am now the master gunner of this town;*
*I must do something to get myself in favour.*
*The Prince's spies have informed me*
*that the English, securely dug in in the suburbs,*
*used a secret grating of iron bars*
*to get into that tower over there to overlook the city,*
*and so to discover the best way*
*they could damage us with shot or attacks.*
*To stop this trouble,*
*I have got a cannon aimed at it;*
*I have been watching the past three days,*
*to see if I could see them.*
*Now you watch, for I can't stop here any longer.*
*If you see anyone, come and tell me,*
*you will find me at the Governor's.*

*[Exit.]*

BOY.
Father, I warrant you; take you no care;
I'll never trouble you, if I may spy them.

*Father, I can promise you; don't you worry;*
*if I can see them, I shan't be troubling you.*

*[Exit.]*

*[Enter, on the turrets, the Lords Salisbury and Talbot, Sir William Glansdale, Sir Thomas Gargrave, and others.]*

SALISBURY.
Talbot, my life, my joy, again return'd!
How wert thou handled being prisoner?
Or by what means got'st thou to be releas'd?
Discourse, I prithee, on this turret's top.

*Talbot, my life, my joy, come back!*
*How were you treated as a prisoner?*
*How did you manage to get released?*
*Come up here, please, and tell me all about it.*

TALBOT.
The Duke of Bedford had a prisoner
Call'd the brave Lord Ponton de Santrailles;
For him was I exchanged and ransomed.
But with a baser man of arms by far
Once in contempt they would have barter'd me:
Which I disdaining scorn'd, and craved death
Rather than I would be so vile-esteem'd.
In fine, redeem'd I was as I desired.

*The Duke of Bedford had a prisoner*
*called the brave Lord Ponton de Satrailles;*
*I was exchanged and ransomed for him.*
*They did want to contemptuously exchange me*
*for far less a soldier at one point,*
*but I disdainfully refused, and said I would rather*
*die than be valued so lowly.*
*So in the end, I got the exchange I wanted.*

But, O! the treacherous Fastolfe wounds my heart,
Whom with my bare fists I would execute,
If I now had him brought into my power.

SALISBURY.
Yet tell'st thou not how thou wert entertain'd.

TALBOT.
With scoffs and scorns and contumelious taunts.
In open market-place produced they me,
To be a public spectacle to all:
Here, said they, is the terror of the French,
The scarecrow that affrights our children so.
Then broke I from the officers that led me,
And with my nails digg'd stones out of the ground
To hurl at the beholders of my shame;
My grisly countenance made others fly;
None durst come near for fear of sudden death.

In iron walls they deem'd me not secure;
So great fear of my name 'mongst them was spread
That they supposed I could rend bars of steel,
And spurn in pieces posts of adamant:
Wherefore a guard of chosen shot I had,
That walk'd about me every minute while;
And if I did but stir out of my bed,
Ready they were to shoot me to the heart.

*[Enter the Boy with a linstock.]*

SALISBURY.
I grieve to hear what torments you endured,
But we will be revenged sufficiently.
Now it is supper-time in Orleans:
Here, through this grate, I count each one,
And view the Frenchmen how they fortify:
Let us look in; the sight will much delight thee.
Sir Thomas Gargrave and Sir William Glansdale,
Let me have your express opinions
Where is best place to make our battery next.

GARGRAVE.
I think, at the north gate; for there stand lords.

GLANSDALE.
And I, here, at the bulwark of the bridge.

TALBOT.
For aught I see, this city must be famish'd,
Or with light skirmishes enfeebled.

*[Here they shoot. Salisbury and Gargrave fall.]*

SALISBURY.
O Lord, have mercy on us, wretched sinners!

---

*But, oh! The treacherous Fastolfe has wounded me,
and I would kill him with my bare hands,
if he was brought to me now.*

*But you haven't said how you were treated.*

*With mockery, scorn and insulting taunts.
They showed me off in the open marketplace,
as a public spectacle:
here, they said, is the terror of the French,
the scarecrow our children are so frightened of.
Then I broke away from the officers who held me,
and with my fingernails I dug stones out of the ground
to throw at those spectators;
my fierce expression made others fly away;
none of them dared come near me in case they should be killed.
They did not think iron bars were enough to hold me;
they were so frightened by my reputation
that they imagined I could tear bars of steel,
and smash rocky door posts to pieces:
so I had a guard of chosen marksmen,
who walked around me every minute of the day;
and if I even just got out of my bed,
they were ready to shoot me through the heart.*

*I'm sorry to hear of the tortures you endured,
but we will soon get adequate revenge.
It's now suppertime in Orleans:
I can see through this grate, I count every person,
and see how the Frenchmen build their defences:
let's have a look; you'll enjoy the sight.
Sir Thomas Gargrave and Sir William Glansdale,
give me your specific opinion
as to where we should direct our next bombardment.*

*I think we should aim at the north gate, there are lords there.*

*I think we should aim at the defences of the bridge.*

*From what I can see, we should starve them out,
or weaken them with repeated small attacks.*

*O Lord, have mercy on us, wretched sinners!*

GARGRAVE.
O Lord, have mercy on me, woful man!

*O Lord, have mercy on me, sorrowful man!*

TALBOT.
What chance is this that suddenly hath cross'd us?
Speak, Salisbury: at least, if thou canst speak:
How farest thou, mirror of all martial men?
One of thy eyes and thy cheek's side struck off!
Accursed tower! accursed fatal hand
That hath contrived this woful tragedy!
In thirteen battles Salisbury o'ercame;
Henry the Fifth he first train'd to the wars;
Whilst any trump did sound, or drum struck up,
His sword did ne'er leave striking in the field.
Yet liv'st thou, Salisbury? though thy speech doth fail,
One eye thou hast, to look to heaven for grace:
The sun with one eye vieweth all the world.
Heaven, be thou gracious to none alive,
If Salisbury wants mercy at thy hands!
Bear hence his body; I will help to bury it,
Sir Thomas Gargrave, hast thou any life?
Speak unto Talbot; nay, look up to him.
Salisbury, cheer thy spirit with this comfort,
Thou shalt not die whiles--
He beckons with his hand and smiles on me,
As who should say 'When I am dead and gone,
Remember to avenge me on the French.'
Plantagenet, I will; and like thee, Nero,
Play on the lute, beholding the towns burn;
Wretched shall France be only in thy name.

*What bit of bad luck have we suddenly had?*
*Speak, Salisbury; at least, speak if you can.*
*How are you, you model soldier?*
*You've lost one of your eyes and the side of your cheek?*
*Damned tower, and damn the fatal hand*
*that caused this terrible tragedy.*
*Salisbury triumphed in thirteen battles:*
*he was the first man to train Henry the Fifth in warfare.*
*He never left off fighting*
*while there were any trumpets sounding or drums beating.*
*Are you still alive, Salisbury? Although you cannot speak,*
*you have one eye to look to heaven for grace.*
*The sun looks at the world with one eye.*
*Heaven, if you don't show mercy to Salisbury*
*then you will show grace to no man alive.*
*Carry his body away—I will help to bury it.*
*Sir Thomas Gargrave, are you still alive?*
*Speak to Talbot, look at him.*
*Salisbury, comfort yourself with this;*
*you won't die while—*
*he signals with his hand and is smiling at me*
*as if he's saying, "when I am dead and gone,*
*make sure you take revenge for me on the French."*
*Plantagenet, I will do so; I'll be like Nero,*
*playing on the lute while he watches the towns burn:*
*France will be terrified just to hear my name.*

[Here an alarum, and it thunders and lightens. ]

What stir is this? what tumult's in the heavens?
Whence cometh this alarum and the noise?

*What's this fuss? What are these storms in the heavens?*
*Where does all this noise and disturbance come from?*

[Enter a Messenger.]

MESSENGER.
My lord, my lord, the French have gather'd head:
The Dauphin, with one Joan la Pucelle join'd,
A holy prophetess new risen up,
Is come with a great power to raise the siege.

*My Lord, the French have formed up for an attack:*
*the Dauphin has come to lift the siege,*
*he has joined forces with one Joan la Pucelle,*
*a newly discovered holy prophetess.*

[Here SALISBURY lifteth himself up and groans.]

TALBOT.
Hear, hear how dying Salisbury doth groan!
It irks his heart he cannot be revenged.
Frenchmen, I 'll be a Salisbury to you:
Pucelle or puzzel, dolphin or dogfish,
Your hearts I 'll stamp out with my horse's heels,
And make a quagmire of your mingled brains.
Convey me Salisbury into his tent,
And then we 'll try what these dastard Frenchmen dare.

*Listen to how the dying Salisbury groans!*
*He hates the fact that he cannot get revenge.*
*Frenchmen, I'll treat you like Salisbury would wish:*
*Pucelle or puzzle, dolphin or dogfish,*
*I'll stamp out your hearts with my horse's heels,*
*and make a swamp of your mixed brains.*
*Carry Salisbury to his tent for me,*
*and then we'll see what these bastard Frenchmen are*
*made of.*

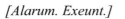

*[Alarum. Exeunt.]*

## SCENE V. The Same.

*[Here an alarum again: and Talbot pursueth the Dauphin, and driveth him: then enter Joan La Pucelle, driving Englishmen before her, and exit after them: then re-enter Talbot.]*

TALBOT.
Where is my strength, my valor, and my force?
Our English troops retire, I cannot stay them:
A woman clad in armour chaseth them.

*What has happened to all my brave forces?*
*The English troops are retreating, I cannot stop them:*
*a woman dressed in armour is chasing them.*

*[Re-enter La Pucelle.]*

Here, here she comes. I 'll have a bout with thee;
Devil or devil's dam, I 'll conjure thee:
Blood will I draw on thee, thou art a witch,
And straightway give thy soul to him thou servest.

*Here she comes. I shall fight you;*
*if you are the Devil or the Devil's mother, I'll beat you:*
*I'll get your blood running, you are a witch,*
*and I'll send back your soul to the one whom you serve.*

PUCELLE.
Come, come, 'tis only I that must disgrace thee.

*Come, come, I must bring you down.*

*[Here they fight.]*

TALBOT.
Heavens, can you suffer hell so to prevail?
My breast I 'll burst with straining of my courage,
And from my shoulders crack my arms asunder,
But I will chastise this high-minded strumpet.

*Heaven, will you allow hell to win like this?*
*I will burst open my chest testing my courage,*
*and let my arms break from my shoulders,*
*but I will punish this arrogant strumpet.*

*[They fight again.]*

PUCELLE.
Talbot, farewell; thy hour is not yet come:
I must go victual Orleans forthwith.

*Talbot, farewell; it's not your time yet:*
*I must go and take supplies to Orleans.*

*[A short alarum: then enter the town with soldiers.]*

O'ertake me, if thou canst; I scorn thy strength.
Go, go, cheer up thy hungry-starved men;
Help Salisbury to make his testament:
This day is ours, as many more shall be.

*Catch me if you can; your strength means nothing to me.*
*Go and cheer up your starving men;*
*help Salisbury to make his will:*
*We have won today, as we shall many other days.*

*[Exit.]*

TALBOT.
My thoughts are whirled like a potter's wheel;
I know not where I am, nor what I do;
A witch, by fear, not force, like Hannibal,
Drives back our troops and conquers as she lists.

*My thoughts are whirling like a potter's wheel:*
*I don't know where I am or what I'm doing.*
*This witch is driving back our troops as Hannibal did,*
*through fear, not through force, and she can do as she likes:*

So bees with smoke and doves with noisome stench
Are from their hives and houses driven away.

*this is the way bees are driven from their hives with smoke,*
*and doves are driven out of their houses with horrible smells.*

They call'd us for our fierceness English dogs;

*Because of our fierceness they called us English dogs;*

Now, like to whelps, we crying run away.
[A short alarum.]

Hark, countrymen!  either renew the fight,
Or tear the lions out of England's coat;
Renounce your soil, give sheep in lions' stead:
Sheep run not half so treacherous from the wolf,
Or horse or oxen from the leopard,
As you fly from your oft-subdued slaves.

[Alarum. Here another skirmish.]

It will not be:  retire into your trenches:
You all consented unto Salisbury's death,
For none would strike a stroke in his revenge.

Pucelle is ent'red into Orleans,
In spite of us or aught that we could do.
O, would I were to die with Salisbury!
The shame hereof will make me hide my head.

[Exit Talbot. Alarum; retreat; flourish.]

*now we are running away like puppies.*

*Listen, countrymen–either go back to the fight
or tear those lions off your English uniforms.
Give up your country, wear sheep badges instead of lions;
sheep don't run so treacherously away from wolves,
or horses or cattle from leopards,
as you are running from this scum you have so often
beaten.*

*It won't happen, retreat to your trenches.
You have all agreed to the death of Salisbury,
because none of you would strike a blow in revenge for
him.
The Maid has gone into Orleans
in spite of us or anything that we could do.
Oh, I wish I could die alongside Salisbury:
the shame of this will make me hide my head.*

## SCENE VI. The Same.

*[Enter, on the walls, La Pucelle, Charles, Reignier, Alencon, and Soldiers.]*

PUCELLE.
Advance our waving colours on the walls;
Rescued is Orleans from the English:
Thus Joan la Pucelle hath perform'd her word.

*Put our banners up on the walls;*
*Orleans has been rescued from the English:*
*and so Joan la Pucelle has kept her word.*

CHARLES.
Divinest creature, Astraea's daughter,
How shall I honour thee for this success?
Thy promises are like Adonis' gardens
That one day bloom'd and fruitful were the next.
France, triumph in thy glorious prophetess!
Recover'd is the town of Orleans.
More blessed hap did ne'er befall our state.

*Most heavenly creature, daughter of Astraea,*
*how can I reward you for this success?*
*Your promises are like the gardens of Adonis,*
*that flowered one day and produced fruit the next.*
*France, rejoice in your glorious prophetess!*
*The town of Orleans has been recaptured.*
*Nothing better than her has ever happened to our country.*

REIGNIER.
Why ring not out the bells aloud throughout the town?
Dauphin, command the citizens make bonfires
And feast and banquet in the open streets,
To celebrate the joy that God hath given us.

*Why not ring out the bells throughout the town?*
*Dauphin, order the citizens to make bonfires*
*and to hold street parties,*
*to celebrate the happiness God has given us.*

ALENCON.
All France will be replete with mirth and joy,
When they shall hear how we have play'd the men.

*All of France will be full of happiness and laughter,*
*when they hear about this brave action.*

CHARLES.
'Tis Joan, not we, by whom the day is won;
For which I will divide my crown with her;
And all the priests and friars in my realm
Shall in procession sing her endless praise.
A statelier pyramis to her I 'll rear
Than Rhodope's of Memphis ever was;
In memory of her when she is dead,
Her ashes, in an urn more precious
Than the rich-jewel'd coffer of Darius,
Transported shall be at high festivals

Before the kings and queens of France.
No longer on Saint Denis will we cry,
But Joan la Pucelle shall be France's saint.
Come in, and let us banquet royally
After this golden day of victory.

*It's Joan, not us, who has won the day;*
*and so I will share my crown with her;*
*and all the priests and monks in my kingdom*
*shall take it in turns to sing her praises eternally.*
*I'll build her a greater pyramid than*
*there ever was in Thrace or at Memphis;*
*when she is dead, in her memory*
*her ashes, in an urn more precious than*
*the richly jewelled treasure chests of Darius,*
*shall be carried in front of the Kings and Queens of France*
*at all the great festivals.*
*We shall no longer appeal to Saint Denis,*
*Joan la Pucelle shall be our saint now.*
*Come inside, and let us have a royal banquet*
*after this golden day of victory.*

*[Flourish. Exeunt.]*

# Act II

## SCENE I. Before Orleans.

*[Enter a Sergeant of a band, with two Sentinels.]*

SERGEANT.
Sirs, take your places and be vigilant:
If any noise or soldier you perceive
Near to the walls, by some apparent sign
Let us have knowledge at the court of guard.

*Sirs, take your places and remain vigilant:*
*if you hear any noise or see any soldiers*
*near to the walls, made some signal*
*to let the guardhouse know.*

FIRST SENTINEL.
Sergeant, you shall. *[Exit Sergeant.]*
Thus are poor servitors,
When others sleep upon their quiet beds,
Constrain'd to watch in darkness, rain and cold.

*Sergeant, we will.*
*So poor common soldiers*
*have to stand out in the rain and cold, in the dark,*
*keeping watch while others sleep in their quiet beds.*

*[Enter Talbot, Bedford, Burgundy, and forces, with scaling-ladders, their drums beating a dead march.]*

TALBOT.
Lord Regent, and redoubted Burgundy,
By whose approach the regions of Artois,
Wallon and Picardy are friends to us,
This happy night the Frenchmen are secure,
Having all day caroused and banqueted:
Embrace we then this opportunity,
As fitting best to quittance their deceit
Contriv'd by art and baleful sorcery.

*Lord Regent, and famed Burgundy,*
*who in joining with us has made the regions of Artois,*
*Wallon and Picardy friendly to us,*
*the Frenchmen are feeling secure tonight,*
*having partied and feasted all day:*
*so let's take this chance as being*
*the best time to pay back their deceit,*
*which was driven by cunning and evil magic.*

BEDFORD.
Coward of France, how much he wrongs his fame,

Despairing of his own arm's fortitude,
To join with witches and the help of hell!

*Cowardly French king, what wrong he does to his own title,*
*so afraid to rely on the strength of his own arm*
*that he has to enlist witches and the assistance of hell!*

BURGUNDY.
Traitors have never other company.
But what 's that Pucelle whom they term so pure?

*That's always been the way with traitors.*
*But who's this Pucelle they call so pure?*

TALBOT.
A maid, they say.

*A girl, they say.*

BEDFORD.
A maid! and be so martial!

*A girl! So soldierly!*

BURGUNDY.
Pray God she prove not masculine ere long,
If underneath the standard of the French
She carry armour as she hath begun.

*I hope she'll stop behaving like a man before long,*
*if she carries on fighting in battle beneath*
*the French standard as she has been.*

TALBOT.
Well, let them practice and converse with spirits:

*Well, let them carry on with their occult practices:*

God is our fortress, in whose conquering name
Let us resolve to scale their flinty bulwarks.

*God is our fortress, and in his conquering name*
*let's climb over their stone battlements.*

BEDFORD.
Ascend, brave Talbot; we will follow thee.

*Climb up, brave Talbot; we will follow you.*

TALBOT.
Not all together:  better far, I guess,
That we do make our entrance several ways;
That, if it chance the one of us do fail,
The other yet may rise against their force.

*Not everyone together: I think it would be far better*
*for us to go in at several different points;*
*that way, if one of us fails,*
*the others can still fight against them.*

BEDFORD.
Agreed:  I 'll to yond corner.

*Agreed: I'll go over to that corner.*

BURGUNDY.
And I to this.

*I'll go to this one.*

TALBOT.
And here will Talbot mount, or make his grave.
Now, Salisbury, for thee, and for the right
Of English Henry, shall this night appear
How much in duty I am bound to both.

*And I will get over here, or die.*
*Now it shall be seen just how much*
*I am prepared to do to do my duty*
*for you, Salisbury, and for the rights of English King*
*Henry.*

SENTINEL.
Arm! arm! the enemy doth make assault!

*Arm yourselves! The enemy is attacking!*

*[Cry: 'St George,' 'A Talbot.']*

*[The French leap over the walls in their shirts. Enter, several ways, the Bastard of Orleans, Alencon, and Reignier, half ready, and half unready.]*

ALENCON.
How now, my lords! what, all unready so?

*What's this, my Lord! What, all so unprepared?*

BASTARD.
Unready! aye, and glad we 'scap'd so well.

*Unprepared! Yes, and glad to have such a lucky escape.*

REIGNIER.
'Twas time, I trow, to wake and leave our beds,
Hearing alarums at our chamber-doors.

*I knew it was time to wake and leave our beds,*
*when I heard the alarm at our bedroom doors.*

ALENCON.
Of all exploits since first I follow'd arms,
Ne'er heard I of a warlike enterprise
More venturous or desperate than this.

*Of all the things I've seen since I became a soldier,*
*I have never heard of anything*
*as adventurous or desperate as this.*

BASTARD.
I think this Talbot be a fiend of hell.

*I think this Talbot is a devil from hell.*

REIGNIER.
If not of hell, the heavens, sure, favor him.

*If he's not from hell, the heavens certainly favour him.*

ALENCON.
Here cometh Charles:  I marvel how he sped.

*Here comes Charles: I'm amazed how quickly he moved.*

BASTARD.
Tut, holy Joan was his defensive guard.

*Well, he had holy Joan to defend him.*

[Enter Charles and La Pucelle.]

CHARLES.
Is this thy cunning, thou deceitful dame?
Didst thou at first, to flatter us withal,
Make us partakers of a little gain,
That now our loss might be ten times so much?

*Is this your cunning plan, you deceitful woman?*
*Did you decide to soften us up*
*by letting us get a little gain,*
*so that now we might lose ten times as much?*

PUCELLE.
Wherefore is Charles impatient with his friend?
At all times will you have my power alike?
Sleeping or waking must I still prevail,
Or will you blame and lay the fault on me?
Improvident soldiers! had your watch been good,
This sudden mischief never could have fall'n.

*Why is Charles so suspicious of his friend?*
*Do you expect my power to be the same at all times?*
*Must I rule everything, sleeping or waking,*
*or are you going to place all the blame on me?*
*Useless soldiers! If you'd kept a good watch,*
*this sudden problem would never have arisen.*

CHARLES.
Duke of Alencon, this was your default,
That, being captain of the watch to-night,
Did look no better to that weighty charge.

*Duke of Alencon, this is your fault,*
*as you were captain of the watch tonight,*
*and you didn't fulfil your responsibility.*

ALENCON.
Had all your quarters been as safely kept
As that whereof I had the government,
We had not been thus shamefully surprised.

*If you'd all guarded your quarters as well*
*as the ones I was guarding,*
*we wouldn't have been caught so shamefully off guard.*

BASTARD.
Mine was secure.

*Mine were secure.*

REIGNIER.
And so was mine, my lord.

*And so were mine, my lord.*

CHARLES.
And, for myself, most part of all this night,
Within her quarter and mine own precinct
I was employ'd in passing to and fro,
About relieving of the sentinels:
Then how or which way should they first break in?

*As for myself I have spent most of this night*
*going to and fro between*
*her quarters and my own,*
*posting sentries:*
*so how and why were they able to break in?*

PUCELLE.
Question, my lords, no further of the case,
How or which way: 'tis sure they found some place
But weakly guarded, where the breach was made.
And now there rests no other shift but this;
To gather our soldiers, scatter'd and dispersed,
And lay new platforms to endamage them.

*My Lords, it no longer matters*
*how or which way: it's certain they found someplace*
*that wasn't properly guarded, where they got in.*
*And now there's nothing else for us to do but this;*
*to gather up our scattered forces*
*and lay down some new plans to harm them.*

[Alarum. Enter an English Soldier, crying 'A Talbot! a Talbot!' They fly, leaving their clothes behind.]

SOLDIER.
I 'll be so bold to take what they have left.
The cry of Talbot serves me for a sword;
For I have loaden me with many spoils,

*I'll be so bold as to take what they've left behind.*
*The cry of "Talbot" is as good as a sword for me;*
*I have got myself plenty of plunder,*

Using no other weapon but his name.                    *just using his name as a weapon.*

[Exit.]

# SCENE II. Orleans. Within the town.

*[Enter Talbot, Bedford, Burgundy, a Captain, and others.]*

BEDFORD.
The day begins to break, and night is fled,
Whose pitchy mantle over-veil'd the earth.
Here sound retreat, and cease our hot pursuit.

*Day begins to break, and night has gone,
removing its dark cloak from the Earth.
Sound the retreat, and end our hot pursuit.*

*[Retreat sounded.]*

TALBOT.
Bring forth the body of old Salisbury,
And here advance it in the market-place,
The middle centre of this cursed town.
Now have I paid my vow unto his soul;
For every drop of blood was drawn from him
There hath at least five Frenchmen died to-night.
And that hereafter ages may behold
What ruin happen'd in revenge of him,
Within their chiefest temple I 'll erect
A tomb, wherein his corpse shall be interr'd;
Upon the which, that every one may read,
Shall be engraved the sack of Orleans,
The treacherous manner of his mournful death
And what a terror he had been to France.
But, lords, in all our bloody massacre,
I muse we met not with the Dauphin's grace,

His new-come champion, virtuous Joan of Arc,
Nor any of his false confederates.

*Bring out the body of old Salisbury,
bring him to the marketplace,
the very centre of this cursed town.
I have now kept my promise to his spirit;
for every drop of blood he shed
at least five Frenchmen died tonight.
And so future generations can see
what destruction there was for his revenge,
I will build him a tomb
inside their greatest church,
and on it, for everyone to read,
I shall have engraved the news of the sack of Orleans,
the treacherous manner of his sad death,
and the terror that he caused to France.
But, lords, in all this bloody massacre,
I'm thinking that we haven't yet come across the Dauphin's
muse,
his newly arrived champion, good Joan of Arc,
or any of his false accomplices.*

BEDFORD.
'Tis thought, Lord Talbot, when the fight began,
Rous'd on the sudden from their drowsy beds,
They did amongst the troops of armed men
Leap o'er the walls for refuge in the field.

*Lord Talbot, it's thought that when the fight began,
having been started from their sleepy beds,
they jumped over the walls with their soldiers,
looking for safety in the field.*

BURGUNDY.
Myself, as far as I could well discern
For smoke and dusky vapors of the night,
Am sure I scared the Dauphin and his trull,
When arm in arm they both came swiftly running,
Like to a pair of loving turtle-doves
That could not live asunder day or night.
After that things are set in order here,
We'll follow them with all the power we have.

*As far as I could make out
through the smoke and the dark of the night,
I'm sure I frightened the Dauphin and his tart,
when they came swiftly running arm in arm
like a pair of loving turtledoves
who can't be separated day or night.
After we get everything in order here,
we'll follow them with all our forces.*

*[Enter a Messenger.]*

MESSENGER.
All hail, my lords! Which of this princely train
Call ye the warlike Talbot, for his acts
So much applauded through the realm of France?

*Greetings, my lords! Who of this princely group
is the warlike Talbot, who is so applauded
for his actions throughout France?*

TALBOT.
Here is the Talbot:  who would speak with him?

*I'm Talbot: who wants to speak to him?*

MESSENGER.
The virtuous lady, Countess of Auvergne,
With modesty admiring thy renown,
By me entreats, great lord, thou wouldst vouchsafe
To visit her poor castle where she lies,
That she may boast she hath beheld the man
Whose glory fills the world with loud report.

*The good lady, Countess of Auvergne,*
*who has been modestly admiring your fame,*
*begs you through me, great Lord, to agree*
*to visit her poor castle where she is staying,*
*so that she can boast that she has seen the man*
*whose glory is so well spoken of throughout the world.*

BURGUNDY.
Is it even so? Nay, then I see our wars
Will turn into a peaceful comic sport,
When ladies crave to be encount'red with.
You may not, my lord, despise her gentle suit.

*Is that so? Well, I see that our wars*
*will become a peaceful comic sport,*
*with ladies desperate to meet us.*
*My lord, you must not reject her polite request.*

TALBOT.
Ne'er trust me then; for when a world of men
Could not prevail with all their oratory,
Yet hath a woman's kindness over-ruled:
And therefore tell her I return great thanks,
And in submission will attend on her.
Will not your honors bear me company?

*You can trust me not to; when the whole world of men*
*couldn't persuade with their speechmaking,*
*a woman's politeness can still win:*
*and so tell her I give my thanks,*
*and I will humbly agree to visit her.*
*Will your honours come with me?*

BEDFORD.
No, truly; it is more than manners will:
And I have heard it said, unbidden guests
Are often welcomest when they are gone.

*Certainly not; that would be bad manners:*
*I've heard it said that uninvited guests*
*are often most welcome when they go.*

TALBOT.
Well then, alone, since there 's no remedy,
I mean to prove this lady's courtesy.
Come hither, Captain.
*[Whispers]* You perceive my mind?

*Well then I'll go alone, if there is no alternative,*
*to test this lady's hospitality.*
*Come here, captain.*
*You know what I'm thinking?*

CAPTAIN.
I do, my lord, and mean accordingly.

*I do, my lord, and I'll do as you say.*

*[Exeunt.]*

# SCENE III. Auvergne. The Countess's castle.

*[Enter the Countess and her Porter.]*

COUNTESS.
Porter, remember what I gave in charge;
And when you have done so, bring the keys to me.

*Porter, remember my orders;*
*when you've carried them out, bring me the keys.*

PORTER.
Madam, I will.

*I will, madam.*

*[Exit.]*

COUNTESS.
The plot is laid: if all things fall out right,
I shall as famous be by this exploit
As Scythian Tomyris by Cyrus' death.
Great is the rumor of this dreadful knight,
And his achievements of no less account:
Fain would mine eyes be witness with mine ears ,
To give their censure of these rare reports.

*The plot is set: if everything works out,*
*I shall be as famous for this exploit*
*as the Scythian Tomyris was for Cyrus' death.*
*This fearsome knight has a great reputation,*
*and it is matched by his achievements:*
*I want my eyes and ears to be witnesses,*
*to give their judgement on these great reports.*

*[Enter Messenger and Talbot.]*

MESSENGER.
Madam,
according as your ladyship desired,
By message craved, so is Lord Talbot come.

*Madam,*
*as your ladyship desired,*
*as you asked in your message, Lord Talbot has come.*

COUNTESS.
And he is welcome. What! is this the man?

*And he is welcome. What! Is this him?*

MESSENGER.
Madam, it is.

*Madam, it is.*

COUNTESS.
Is this the scourge of France?
Is this the Talbot, so much fear'd abroad
That with his name the mothers still their babes?
I see report is fabulous and false:
I thought I should have seen some Hercules,
A second Hector, for his grim aspect,
And large proportion of his strong-knit limbs.
Alas, this is a child, a silly dwarf!
It cannot be this weak and writhled shrimp
Should strike such terror to his enemies.

*Is this the one who has whipped France?*
*Is this Talbot, who is so feared around the country*
*that his mothers use his name to quiet their babies?*
*I see the stories are mythical and false:*
*I thought I would have seen some Hercules,*
*a second Hector, in his stern looks,*
*and his great muscular limbs.*
*Alas, this is a child, a silly dwarf!*
*This weak and wrinkled shrimp can't possibly*
*strike such fear into his enemies.*

TALBOT.
Madam, I have been bold to trouble you;
But since your ladyship is not at leisure,
I 'll sort some other time to visit you.

*Madam, I have been forward enough to bother you;*
*but since you are not free at the moment,*
*I'll come and see you some other time.*

COUNTESS.
What means he now? Go ask him whither he goes.

*Now what's he mean? Asking where he's going.*

MESSENGER.
Stay, my Lord Talbot; for my lady craves
To know the cause of your abrupt departure.

*Wait, my Lord Talbot; my lady wants*
*to know why you are leaving so suddenly.*

TALBOT.
Marry, for that she's in a wrong belief,
I go to certify her Talbot's here.

*Why, because she's completely wrong,*
*I'm going to prove to her that Talbot is here.*

*[Re-enter Porter with keys.]*

COUNTESS.
If thou be he, then art thou prisoner.

*If you're him, then you are prisoner.*

TALBOT.
Prisoner! to whom?

*Prisoner! Of whom?*

COUNTESS.
To me, blood-thirsty lord;
And for that cause I train'd thee to my house.
Long time thy shadow hath been thrall to me,
For in my gallery thy picture hangs:
But now the substance shall endure the like,
And I will chain these legs and arms of thine,
That hast by tyranny these many years
Wasted our country, slain our citizens,
And sent our sons and husbands captive.

*Of me, bloodthirsty lord;*
*that was why I enticed you to my house.*
*For a long time your image has been my slave,*
*for I have your picture in my gallery:*
*but now the real thing shall be the same,*
*and I will chain those arms and legs of yours,*
*that through your tyranny for many years*
*have laid waste to our country, killed our citizens,*
*and imprisoned our sons and husbands.*

TALBOT.
Ha, ha, ha!

*Ha, ha, ha!*

COUNTESS.
Laughest thou, wretch? Thy mirth shall turn to moan.

*Are you laughing, wretch? Your laughter shall turn to*
*moaning.*

TALBOT.
I laugh to see your ladyship so fond
To think that you have aught but Talbot's shadow

Whereon to practice your severity.

*I'm laughing to see that your ladyship is so foolish*
*that you think you have anything apart from Talbot's*
*image*
*on which you can practice your punishments.*

COUNTESS.
Why, art not thou the man?

*Why, aren't you the man?*

TALBOT.
I am indeed.

*I certainly am.*

COUNTESS.
Then have I substance too.

*Then I have the real thing too.*

TALBOT.
No, no, I am but shadow of myself:
You are deceived, my substance is not here;
For what you see is but the smallest part
And least proportion of humanity:
I tell you, madam, were the whole frame here,
It is of such a spacious lofty pitch,
Your roof were not sufficient to contain 't.

*No, no, I am just a shadow of myself:*
*you are mistaken you're not seeing the real thing;*
*what you can see is just the smallest part,*
*with the least humanity in it:*
*I tell you, madam, if the whole of me were here,*
*it is so enormous*
*your roof wouldn't be able to hold it.*

COUNTESS.
This is a riddling merchant for the nonce;
He will be here, and yet he is not here:
How can these contrarieties agree?

*You are talking in riddles;*
*you are here, but you're not here:*
*how can those two opposites make sense?*

TALBOT.
That will I show you presently.

*I'll show you that now.*

*[Winds his horn. Drums strike up: a peal of ordnance. Enter Soldiers.]*

How say you, madam? are you now persuaded
That Talbot is but shadow of himself?
These are his substance, sinews, arms and strength,
With which he yoketh your rebellious necks,
Razeth your cities and subverts your towns,
And in a moment makes them desolate.

*What do you say, madam? Do you now believe*
*that Talbot is just a shadow of himself?*
*These are my body, muscles, arms and strength,*
*with which I have been chaining your rebellious necks,*
*destroying your cities and towns,*
*making them desolate in an instant.*

COUNTESS.
Victorious Talbot! pardon my abuse:
I find thou art no less than fame hath bruited,
And more than may be gather'd by thy shape.
Let my presumption not provoke thy wrath;
For I am sorry that with reverence
I did not entertain thee as thou art.

*Victorious Talbot! Excuse my ill-treatment:*
*I find you are just as great as your reputation,*
*and that there's more to you than meets the eye.*
*Don't let my assumptions make you angry;*
*I'm sorry that I didn't show you the respect*
*of treating you as the person you are.*

TALBOT.
Be not dismay'd, fair lady; nor misconstrue
The mind of Talbot, as you did mistake
The outward composition of his body.
What you have done hath not offended me;
Nor other satisfaction do I crave,
But only, with your patience, that we may
Taste of your wine and see what cates you have;
For soldiers' stomachs always serve them well.

*Don't worry about it, fair lady; and don't misunderstand*
*the mind of Talbot, as you mistook*
*the way his body was made.*
*What you have done has not offended me;*
*I don't want any recompense,*
*except that, with your permission, we should like*
*to taste your wine and try your food;*
*soldiers are always hungry.*

COUNTESS.
With all my heart, and think me honored
To feast so great a warrior in my house.

*Certainly, and I would count it an honour*
*to feed such a great warrior in my house.*

*[Exeunt.]*

# SCENE IV. London. The Temple-garden.

*[Enter the Earls of Somerset, Suffolk, and Warwick; Richard Plantagenet, Vernon, and another Lawyer.]*

PLANTAGENET.
Great lords and gentlemen,
what means this silence?
Dare no man answer in a case of truth?

*Great lords and gentlemen,*
*why are you silent?*
*Can nobody give us the truth?*

SUFFOLK.
Within the Temple-hall we were too loud;
The garden here is more convenient.

*We were too noisy in the Temple Hall;*
*this garden is more suitable.*

PLANTAGENET.
Then say at once if I maintain'd the truth;
Or else was wrangling Somerset in the error?

*Then say at once if what I said was true,*
*or was the argumentative Somerset wrong?*

SUFFOLK.
Faith, I have been a truant in the law,
And never yet could frame my will to it;
And therefore frame the law unto my will.

*I swear, I have been lax in learning the law,*
*I can never really understand it,*
*and therefore I can't make it do what I want.*

SOMERSET.
Judge you, my Lord of Warwick, then, between us.

*Then you judge, Lord Warwick, between us.*

WARWICK.
Between two hawks, which flies the higher pitch;
Between two dogs, which hath the deeper mouth;
Between two blades, which bears the better temper:
Between two horses, which doth bear him best;
Between two girls, which hath the merriest eye;
I have perhaps some shallow spirit of judgment:
But in these nice sharp quillets of the law,
Good faith, I am no wiser than a daw.

*I can probably judge*
*between two hawks, which one can fly higher;*
*between two dogs, which has the bigger mouth;*
*between two swords, which one is better made:*
*between two horses, which one will be the best ride;*
*between two girls, who has the sauciest look;*
*but in these subtle distinctions of legal language*
*I swear, I am no wiser than a jackdaw.*

PLANTAGENET.
Tut, tut, here is a mannerly forbearance:
The truth appears so naked on my side
That any purblind eye may find it out.

*Tut tut, you're just being polite:*
*it's so obvious that truth is on my side*
*that the blindest man could see it.*

SOMERSET.
And on my side it is so well apparell'd,
So clear, so shining and so evident,
That it will glimmer through a blind man's eye.

*And it's so obvious on my side,*
*so clear and so bright,*
*that a blind man could see it shining.*

PLANTAGENET.
Since you are tongue-tied and so loath to speak,
In dumb significants proclaim your thoughts:
Let him that is a true-born gentleman
And stands upon the honor of his birth,
If he suppose that I have pleaded truth,
From off this brier pluck a white rose with me.

*Since you are tongue tied and don't wish to speak,*
*you can show your thoughts in sign language.*
*That person who is a true born gentleman*
*and has faith in his noble birth,*
*if he thinks that I have spoken the truth,*
*let him pick a white rose from this bush with me.*

SOMERSET.
Let him that is no coward nor no flatterer,

*Let the one who is not a coward or flatterer,*

But dare maintain the party of the truth,
Pluck a red rose from off this thorn with me.

*who dares to stick to the truth,*
*pick a red rose from this bush with me.*

WARWICK.
I love no colours, and without all colour
Of base insinuating flattery
I pluck this white rose with Plantagenet.

*I don't like taking sides,*
*but without any sort of low motives*
*I shall pluck this white rose with Plantagenet.*

SUFFOLK.
I pluck this red rose with young Somerset,
And say withal I think he held the right.

*I shall pluck this red rose with young Somerset,*
*and furthermore say I think he was in the right.*

VERNON.
Stay, lords and gentlemen, and pluck no more,
Till you conclude that he, upon whose side
The fewest roses are cropp'd from the tree
Shall yield the other in the right opinion.

*Wait, lords and gentlemen, and pick no more,*
*until you have agreed that the person who has*
*the fewest roses picked from the tree*
*should accept the other is in the right.*

SOMERSET.
Good Master Vernon, it is well objected:
If I have fewest, I subscribe in silence.

*Good Master Vernon, you're quite right:*
*if I have the fewest, I shall give in without speaking.*

PLANTAGENET.
And I.

*I agree.*

VERNON.
Then for the truth and plainness of the case,
I pluck this pale and maiden blossom here,
Giving my verdict on the white rose side.

*Then for the obvious truth of the case,*
*I shall pluck this pale and virginal blossom,*
*giving my judgement on the side of the white rose.*

SOMERSET.
Prick not your finger as you pluck it off,
Lest bleeding, you do paint the white rose red,
And fall on my side so, against your will.

*Don't prick your finger as you pick it,*
*in case you bleed and paint the white rose red,*
*and fall on my side, against your will.*

VERNON.
If I, my lord, for my opinion bleed,
Opinion shall be surgeon to my hurt
And keep me on the side where still I am.

*If I am to bleed for my opinion, my lord,*
*my opinion shall be my doctor*
*and keep me on the side I've chosen.*

SOMERSET.
Well, well, come on:  who else?

*Very good, come on: who else?*

LAWYER.
Unless my study and my books be false,
The argument you held was wrong in you;

*Unless my studying and my books are wrong,*
*your argument was mistaken;*

[To Somerset.]

In sign whereof I pluck a white rose too.

*and so I pick a white rose too.*

PLANTAGENET.
Now, Somerset, where is your argument?

*Now, Somerset, where is your case?*

SOMERSET.
Here in my scabbard, meditating that

*Here in my scabbard, thinking of ways*

Shall dye your white rose in a bloody red.

PLANTAGENET.
Meantime your cheeks do counterfeit our roses;
For pale they look with fear, as witnessing
The truth on our side.

SOMERSET.
No, Plantagenet,
'Tis not for fear but anger that thy cheeks
Blush for pure shame to counterfeit our roses,
And yet thy tongue will not confess thy error.

PLANTAGENET.
Hath not thy rose a canker, Somerset?

SOMERSET.
Hath not thy rose a thorn, Plantagenet?

PLANTAGENET.
Ay, sharp and piercing, to maintain his truth;
Whiles thy consuming canker eats his falsehood.

SOMERSET.
Well, I 'll find friends to wear my bleeding roses,
That shall maintain what I have said is true,
Where false Plantagenet dare not be seen.

PLANTAGENET.
Now, by this maiden blossom in my hand,
I scorn thee and thy fashion, peevish boy.

SUFFOLK.
Turn not thy scorns this way, Plantagenet.

PLANTAGENET.
Proud Pole, I will, and scorn both him and thee.

SUFFOLK.
I'll turn my part thereof into thy throat.

SOMERSET.
Away, away, good William de la Pole!
We grace the yeoman by conversing with him.

WARWICK.
Now, by God's will, thou wrong'st him, Somerset;
His grandfather was Lionel Duke of Clarence,
Third son to the third Edward King of England:
Spring crestless yeomen from so deep a root?

PLANTAGENET.
He bears him on the place's privilege,
Or durst not, for his craven heart, say thus.

SOMERSET.

---

*I can dye your white rose bloody red.*

*In the meantime your cheeks imitate our roses;*
*they look pale with fear, having seen*
*the truth on our side.*

*No, Plantagenet,*
*it is not out of fear but anger, seeing your cheeks*
*blush with shame to imitate our roses,*
*but your tongue will not admit you are wrong.*

*Hasn't your rose some disease, Somerset?*

*Hasn't your rose got a thorn, Plantagenet?*

*Yes, sharp and piercing, to uphold his truth;*
*while your disease eats its own leaves.*

*Well, I shall find friends who will wear my bleeding roses,*
*who will agree that what I have said is true,*
*in places where false Plantagenet dare not show his face.*

*Now, by this virginal blossom in my hand,*
*I reject you and your sort, miserable boy.*

*Don't be so scornful, Plantagenet.*

*Proud Pole, I shall, and I scorn you and him.*

*I'll shove my share of that back down your throat.*

*Come away, good William de la Pole!*
*We're giving this peasant too much honour by talking to*
*him.*

*Now, I swear, you are insulting him, Somerset;*
*his grandfather was Lionel Duke of Clarence,*
*the third son of Edward the Third, King of England:*
*do unmarked peasants spring from such heritage?*

*He's relying on the laws of this place,*
*or otherwise, coward that he is, he wouldn't dare say it.*

By Him that made me, I'll maintain my words
On any plot of ground in Christendom.
Was not thy father, Richard Earl of Cambridge,
For treason executed in our late king's days?
And, by his treason, stand'st not thou attainted,
Corrupted, and exempt from ancient gentry?
His trespass yet lives guilty in thy blood;
And, till thou be restored, thou art a yeoman.

PLANTAGENET.
My father was attached, not attainted,
Condemn'd to die for treason, but no traitor;
And that I'll prove on better men than Somerset,
Were growing time once ripen'd to my will.
For your partaker Pole and you yourself,
I'll note you in my book of memory,
To scourge you for this apprehension:
Look to it well and say you are well warn'd.

SOMERSET.
Ay, thou shalt find us ready for thee still;
And know us by these colors for thy foes,
For these my friends in spite of thee shall wear.

PLANTAGENET.
And, by my soul, this pale and angry rose,
As cognizance of my blood-drinking hate,
Will I for ever and my faction wear,
Until it wither with me to my grave,
Or flourish to the height of my degree.

SUFFOLK.
Go forward, and be chok'd with thy ambition!
And so farewell until I meet thee next.

[Exit.]

SOMERSET.
Have with thee, Pole. Farewell, ambitious Richard.

[Exit.]

PLANTAGENET.
How I am braved and must perforce endure it!

WARWICK.
This blot that they object against your house
Shall be wiped out in the next parliament
Call'd for the truce of Winchester and Gloucester;

And if thou be not then created York,
I will not live to be accounted Warwick.
Meantime, in signal of my love to thee,
Against proud Somerset and William Pole,
Will I upon thy party wear this rose:
And here I prophesy:  this brawl to-day,

*By God, I'll say this*
*on any piece of ground in Christendom.*
*Wasn't your father, Richard Earl of Cambridge,*
*executed for treason in  the days of our late King?*
*And, due to his treason, haven't you lost your rights,*
*your place amongst the old noble families?*
*His sin is still living in your blood;*
*and until you're given your place back, you are a peasant.*

*My father was arrested, not penalised,*
*condemned to die for treason, but not a traitor;*
*and I'll prove that to better men than Somerset,*
*if time allows me.*
*As for your accomplice Pole and you yourself,*
*I'll make a mental note*
*to punish you for your attacks:*
*remember it and don't complain you haven't been warned.*

*Yes and you will find we're ready for you;*
*you'll know we're your enemies from our colours,*
*which my friends shall wear, in spite of you.*

*And I swear, in recognition of my bloodthirsty hate,*
*myself and my party will always*
*wear this pale and angry rose,*
*until it dies with me in my grave,*
*or grows along with my rank.*

*Off you go, and may your ambition choke you!*
*And so farewell until I see you next.*

*Enough of you, Pole. Farewell, ambitious Richard.*

*What challenges I have to put up with!*

*This stain that they say is on your house*
*shall be wiped out in the next Parliament,*
*that was called for the truce between Winchester and*
*Gloucester;*
*and if you are not then made Duke of York,*
*then I shall not be called Warwick.*
*Meanwhile, as a sign of my love for you,*
*against proud Somerset and William Pole,*
*I shall wear this rose for your party:*
*and I predict this: this brawl today,*

Grown to this faction in the Temple-garden,

Shall send between the red rose and the white
A thousand souls to death and deadly night.

PLANTAGENET.
Good Master Vernon, I am bound to you,
That you on my behalf would pluck a flower.

VERNON.
In your behalf still will I wear the same.

LAWYER.
And so will I.

PLANTAGENET.
Thanks, gentle sir.
Come, let us four to dinner:  I dare say
This quarrel will drink blood another day.

*[Exeunt.]*

*which grew to become this disagreement in the Temple
garden,*
*shall, between the red rose and the white,*
*mean the death of a thousand souls.*

*Good Master Vernon, I am obliged to you,*
*that you would pick a flower on my behalf.*

*I shall wear it on your behalf.*

*And so will I.*

*Thank you, kind sir.*
*Come, let the four of us go to dinner: I dare say*
*blood will be spilt over this quarrel some other day.*

# SCENE V. The Tower of London.

*[Enter Mortimer, brought in a chair, and Jailers.]*

MORTIMER.
Kind keepers of my weak decaying age,
Let dying Mortimer here rest himself.
Even like a man new haled from the rack,
So fare my limbs with long imprisonment;
And these gray locks, the pursuivants of death,
Nestor-like aged in an age of care,
Argue the end of Edmund Mortimer.
These eyes, like lamps whose wasting oil is spent,
Wax dim, as drawing to their exigent;
Weak shoulders, overborne with burdening grief,
And pithless arms, like to a wither'd vine
That droops his sapless branches to the ground:
Yet are these feet, whose strengthless stay is numb,
Unable to support this lump of clay,
Swift-winged with desire to get a grave,
As witting I no other comfort have.
But tell me, keeper, will my nephew come?

*Kind guardians of my weakened fading age,*
*let the dying Mortimer have a rest here.*
*Long imprisonment has made my limbs feel like*
*those of a man just pulled off the rack;*
*and these grey hairs, the forerunners of death,*
*aged like Nestor through ages of care,*
*say that the end of Edmund Mortimer is near.*
*These eyes, like lamps whose oil is running out,*
*grow dim, reaching their end;*
*weak shoulders, overloaded with grief,*
*and feeble arms, like a shrivelled vine*
*that trails its dead branches along the ground:*
*both these feet, which are numb and unsupportive,*
*and cannot support this lump of clay,*
*are filled with the desire to speed to the grave,*
*knowing that it will be my only comfort.*
*But tell me, jailer, will my nephew come?*

FIRST JAILER.
Richard Plantagenet, my lord, will come:
We sent unto the Temple, unto his chamber;
And answer was return'd that he will come.

*Richard Plantagenet will come, my lord:*
*we sent messages to the Temple, to his rooms;*
*and he returned the answer that he will come.*

MORTIMER.
Enough:  my soul shall then be satisfied.
Poor gentleman! his wrong doth equal mine.

Since Henry Monmouth first began to reign,
Before whose glory I was great in arms,
This loathsome sequestration have I had;
And even since then hath Richard been obscured,
Deprived of honour and inheritance.
But now the arbitrator of despairs,
Just Death, kind umpire of men's miseries,
With sweet enlargement doth dismiss me hence:
I would his troubles likewise were expired,
That so he might recover what was lost.

*That's enough for me, my soul will then be happy.*
*Poor gentleman! The wrongs done to him are the equal of*
*mine.*
*Since Henry Monmouth began his reign*
*(before his ascendancy I was a great soldier)*
*I have been locked away in this horrible fashion;*
*and since that time Richard has been overlooked,*
*deprived of his titles and his inheritance.*
*But now the arbitrator of sorrow,*
*Just Death, the kind umpire of men's misery,*
*will give me my freedom and take me from here:*
*I wish his troubles were over for him,*
*so that he might get back what has been lost.*

*[Enter Richard Plantagenet.]*

FIRST JAILER.
My lord, your loving nephew now is come.

*My lord, your loving nephew has now come.*

MORTIMER.
Richard Plantagenet, my friend, is he come?

*Has Richard Plantagenet, my friend, come?*

PLANTAGENET.
Aye, noble uncle, thus ignobly used,
Your nephew, late despised Richard, comes.

*Yes, noble uncle, who has been so poorly treated,*
*your nephew, the recently despised Richard, has come.*

MORTIMER.
Direct mine arms I may embrace his neck,
And in his bosom spend my latter gasp:
O, tell me when my lips do touch his cheeks,
That I may kindly give one fainting kiss.
And now declare, sweet stem from York's great stock,
Why didst thou say of late thou wert despised?

*Move my arms so that I may embrace him,*
*and die with my head on his chest:*
*oh, tell me when my lips touch his cheeks,*
*so that I can give him one last weak family kiss.*
*Now tell me, sweet offshoot of the great tree of York,*
*why did you say that you were despised at the moment?*

PLANTAGENET.
First, lean thine aged back against mine arm;
And, in that case, I'll tell thee my disease.
This day, in argument upon a case,
Some words there grew 'twixt Somerset and me;

Among which terms he used his lavish tongue
And did upbraid me with my father's death:
Which obloquy set bars before my tongue,
Else with the like I had requited him.
Therefore, good uncle, for my father's sake,
In honor of a true Plantagenet
And for alliance sake, declare the cause
My father, Earl of Cambridge, lost his head.

*Firstly, lean your old back against my arm;*
*and, when you've done that, I'll tell you my problem.*
*Today, arguing over a legal case,*
*there was an exchange of words between myself and Somerset;*
*during this he used his extravagant tongue*
*to make remarks about my father's death:*
*this slander rendered me speechless,*
*otherwise I would have paid him back in the same kind.*
*Therefore, good uncle, for my father's sake,*
*for the honour of a true Plantagenet,*
*and for the sake of family loyalty, tell me the reason*
*my father, Earl of Cambridge, was beheaded.*

MORTIMER.
That cause, fair nephew, that imprison'd me

And hath detain'd me all my flowering youth
Within a loathsome dungeon, there to pine,
Was cursed instrument of his decease.

*The same reason, fair nephew, that I have been imprisoned,*
*and have spent my entire youth*
*inside a horrid dungeon, to pine away,*
*that is what killed him.*

PLANTAGENET.
Discover more at large what cause that was,
For I am ignorant and cannot guess.

*Give me more details as to the reason,*
*for I do not know and I cannot guess.*

MORTIMER.
I will, if that my fading breath permit,
And death approach not ere my tale be done.
Henry the Fourth, grandfather to this king,
Deposed his nephew Richard, Edward's son,
The first-begotten and the lawful heir
Of Edward king, the third of that descent;
During whose reign the Percies of the north,
Finding his usurpation most unjust,
Endeavour'd my advancement to the throne.
The reason moved these warlike lords to this
Was, for that--young King Richard thus removed,
Leaving no heir begotten of his body--
I was the next by birth and parentage;
For by my mother I derived am
From Lionel Duke of Clarence, third son
To King Edward the Third; whereas he
From John of Gaunt doth bring his pedigree,
Being but fourth of that heroic line.
But mark: as in this haughty great attempt
They labored to plant the rightful heir,
I lost my liberty and they their lives.

*I will, if my failing breath allows me,*
*and death does not take me before my story is finished.*
*Henry the Fourth, grandfather of the current king,*
*overthrew his nephew Richard, the son of Edward,*
*the firstborn and the lawful heir*
*of Edward, the third King in that line,*
*and during his reign the Percys of the North,*
*thinking his overthrow extremely unjust,*
*attempted to place me on the throne.*
*The reason these warlike lords had for this was*
*that--with young Richard dead,*
*leaving no direct heir--*
*I was next in line through birth and ancestry:*
*for on my mother's side I am descended*
*from Lionel, Duke of Clarence, third son*
*of King Edward the Third, whereas he*
*is descended from John of Gaunt,*
*only fourth in that heroic genealogy.*
*But you can see that in this noble great attempt*
*at installing the rightful heir on the throne*
*I lost my freedom and they lost their lives.*

| Original | Modern |
|---|---|
| Long after this, when Henry the Fifth, / Succeeding his father Bolingbroke, did reign, / Thy father, Earl of Cambridge, then derived / From famous Edmund Langley, Duke of York, / Marrying my sister that thy mother was, / Again in pity of my hard distress. / Levied an army, weening to redeem / And have install'd me in the diadem: / But, as the rest, so fell that noble earl / And was beheaded. Thus the Mortimers, / In whom the title rested, were suppress'd. | Long after this, when Henry the Fifth, / succeeding his father Bolingbroke, ruled, / your father, then Earl of Cambridge–descended / from famous Edmund Langley, Duke of York– / married my sister, your mother, / and again, out of pity at my horrid predicament, / raised an army, intending to free me / and give me the Crown. / But that noble Earl failed like the rest, / and was beheaded. So the Mortimers, / who have the right to the title, were suppressed. |

PLANTAGENET.

| Original | Modern |
|---|---|
| Of which, my lord, your honor is the last. | And you are the last of them, my lord. |

MORTIMER.

| Original | Modern |
|---|---|
| True; and thou seest that I no issue have, / And that my fainting words do warrant death: / Thou art my heir; the rest I wish thee gather: / / But yet be wary in thy studious care. | True, and you see I have no children, / and that my halting words show I am dying: / you are my heir; I want you to think about what that means: / but be careful what you do with your discoveries. |

PLANTAGENET.

| Original | Modern |
|---|---|
| Thy grave admonishments prevail with me: / But yet, methinks, my father's execution / Was nothing less than bloody tyranny. | Your grave warnings will be noted: / but still, I think that my father's execution / was nothing less than the act of a bloody tyrant. |

MORTIMER.

| Original | Modern |
|---|---|
| With silence, nephew, be thou politic: / Strong-fixed is the house of Lancaster, / And like a mountain not to be removed. / But now thy uncle is removing hence; / As princes do their courts, when they are cloy'd / / With long continuance in a settled place. | Make sure you keep a diplomatic silence, nephew: / the house of Lancaster is firmly fixed, / and you might as well try to move a mountain. / But now your uncle is moving from here; / in the same way that Princes move their courts, when they are bored / by staying too long in one place. |

PLANTAGENET.

| Original | Modern |
|---|---|
| O, uncle, would some part of my young years / Might but redeem the passage of your age! | Oh, uncle, if only I could give some of my youth / to take away some of your age! |

MORTIMER.

| Original | Modern |
|---|---|
| Thou dost then wrong me, as that slaughterer doth / Which giveth many wounds when one will kill. / Mourn not, except thou sorrow for my good; / Only give order for my funeral: / And so farewell, and fair be all thy hopes, / And prosperous be thy life in peace and war! | Then you would be harming me, like a slaughterer who / gives many wounds when one would do for killing. / Do not mourn, except for sorrow at any good in me; / just arrange my funeral. / And so farewell, and may you be successful / and prosperous in peace and in war! |

[Dies.]

PLANTAGENET.

| Original | Modern |
|---|---|
| And peace, no war, befall thy parting soul! / In prison hast thou spent a pilgrimage, / And like a hermit overpass'd thy days. / Well, I will lock his counsel in my breast; / And what I do imagine let that rest. | And may peace, not war, come to your departing soul! / You have spent the time of a pilgrimage in prison, / and like a hermit you have lived beyond your time. / Well, I shall lock his advice away in my heart; / and let my imagination rest for the moment. |

Keepers, convey him hence; and I myself
Will see his burial better than his life.

*[Exeunt Jailers, bearing out the body of Mortimer.]*

Here dies the dusky torch of Mortimer,
Choked with ambition of the meaner sort:
And for those wrongs, those bitter injuries,
Which Somerset hath offer'd to my house,
I doubt not but with honour to redress;
And therefore haste I to the parliament,
Either to be restored to my blood,
Or make my will the advantage of my good.

*[Exit.]*

*Jailers, take him away; I myself*
*will make sure he is treated better in death than he was in*
*life.*

*Here dies the failing torch of Mortimer,*
*extinguished by the ambition of lower men:*
*and for those wrongs, those bitter insults,*
*which Somerset offered to my family,*
*I do not doubt I shall honourably punish them;*
*and therefore I hurry to the Parliament,*
*either to be given back my rightful place,*
*or to assert my will to get what I deserve.*

# Act III

## SCENE I. London. The Parliament-house.

*[Flourish. Enter King, Exeter, Gloucester, Warwick, Somerset, and Suffolk; the Bishop of Winchester, Richard Plantagenet, and others. Gloucester offers to put up a bill; Winchester snatches it, tears it.]*

WINCHESTER.
Comest thou with deep premeditated lines,
With written pamphlets studiously devised,
Humphrey of Gloucester?  If thou canst accuse,
Or aught intend'st to lay unto my charge.
Do it without invention, suddenly;
As I with sudden and extemporal speech
Purpose to answer what thou canst object.

*Have you come with a preplanned text,*
*carefully written long thought out pamphlets,*
*Humphrey of Gloucester? If you have accusations,*
*or intend to charge me with anything,*
*do it at once, don't use your rhetorical style;*
*I intend to answer your accusations*
*immediately, off-the-cuff.*

GLOUCESTER.
Presumptuous priest! this place commands my patience,
Or thou shouldst find thou hast dishonor'd me.
Think not, although in writing I preferr'd
The manner of thy vile outrageous crimes,
That therefore I have forged, or am not able
Verbatim to rehearse the method of my pen:
No, prelate; such is thy audacious wickedness,
Thy lewd, pestiferous and dissentious pranks,
As very infants prattle of thy pride.
Thou art a most pernicious usurer,
Froward by nature, enemy to peace;
Lascivious, wanton, more than well beseems
A man of thy profession and degree;
And for thy treachery, what's more manifest
In that thou laid'st a trap to take my life,
As well at London-bridge as at the Tower.
Beside, I fear me, if thy thoughts are sifted
The king, thy sovereign, is not quite exempt
From envious malice of thy swelling heart.

*Arrogant priest, this place demands I keep calm,*
*or you would be punished for your insult.*
*Do not think that just because I wrote down*
*the details of your revolting terrible crimes*
*that I have made anything up or cannot*
*repeat orally what I have written.*
*No, bishop, such is your blatant wickedness,*
*your lecherous, dirty and disloyal goings on,*
*that even children talk about your arrogance.*
*You are an evil moneylender,*
*perverse by nature, an enemy to peace,*
*lusty and profligate–more than suits*
*a man of your calling and rank.*
*As for your treachery, what could be more obvious*
*than that you laid traps to take my life,*
*at London Bridge as well as at the Tower?*
*Also, I'm afraid, if your thoughts could be read,*
*the King, your sovereign, does not quite escape*
*the envious malice in your puffed up heart.*

WINCHESTER.
Gloucester, I do defy thee. Lords, vouchsafe
To give me hearing what I shall reply.
If I were covetous, ambitious, or perverse,
As he will have me, how am I so poor?
Or how haps it I seek not to advance
Or raise myself, but keep my wonted calling?
And for dissension, who preferreth peace
More than I do?--except I be provoked.
No, my good lords, it is not that offends;
It is not that that hath incensed the duke:
It is, because no one should sway but he;
No one but he should be about the king;
And that engenders thunder in his breast,
And makes him roar these accusations forth.
But he shall know I am as good--

*Gloucester, I spurn you. Lords, do me the honour*
*of listening to my reply.*
*If I were covetous, ambitious or perverse,*
*as he accuses, why am I so poor?*
*Why have I not tried to advance*
*or promote myself, but kept to my usual vocation?*
*As for dissent, who prefers peace*
*more than I do?–Unless I am provoked.*
*No, my good lords, it is not that that has caused offence;*
*it is not that that has angered the Duke:*
*it is, because he wants no want to have power but him;*
*no one but him should be around the King;*
*and that makes the thunder brew up in his breast,*
*and makes him shout out these accusations.*
*But he will know that I am as good–*

GLOUCESTER.
As good!
Thou bastard of my grandfather!

WINCHESTER.
Aye, lordly sir; for what are you, I pray,
But one imperious in another's throne?

GLOUCESTER.
Am I not protector, saucy priest?

WINCHESTER.
And am not I a prelate of the church?

GLOUCESTER.
Yes, as an outlaw in a castle keeps
And useth it to patronage his theft.

WINCHESTER.
Unreverent Gloster!

GLOUCESTER.
Thou art reverent
Touching thy spiritual function, not thy life.

WINCHESTER.
Rome shall remedy this.

WARWICK.
Roam thither, then.

SOMERSET.
My lord, it were your duty to forbear.

WARWICK.
Ay, see the bishop be not overborne.

SOMERSET.
Methinks my lord should be religious,
And know the office that belongs to such.

WARWICK.
Methinks his lordship should be humbler;
It fitteth not a prelate so to plead.

SOMERSET.
Yes, when his holy state is touch'd so near.

WARWICK.
State holy or unhallow'd, what of that?
Is not his grace protector to the king?

PLANTAGENET.
[Aside] Plantagenet, I see, must hold his tongue,
Lest it be said, 'Speak, sirrah, when you should:

*As good!*
*You bastard of my grandfather!*

*Yes, lordly sir; and what are you, tell me,*
*but someone who plays the King on another's throne?*

*Am I not the Regent, cheeky priest?*

*And am I not a Bishop of the church?*

*Yes, like an outlaw who stays in a castle*
*and uses it to help his thievery.*

*Irreverent Gloucester!*

*You are reverent*
*when doing your spiritual job, not in your life.*

*Rome shall make you pay for this.*

*Go there then.*

*My lord, you really must stop this.*

*Yes, make sure the Bishop is not oppressed.*

*I think my lord should be religious,*
*and show the respect religious men deserve.*

*I think his Lordship should be more humble:*
*it's not right for a Bishop to be accused like this.*

*Yes, putting his holy status so much in question.*

*If his status is holy or unholy, what of it?*
*Isn't his grace the King's Regent?*

*I see that Plantagenet must hold his tongue,*
*otherwise they'll say, "Speak, lad, when you're spoken to:*

Must your bold verdict enter talk with lords?'

Else would I have a fling at Winchester.

KING.
Uncles of Gloucester and of Winchester,
The special watchmen of our English weal,
I would prevail, if prayers might prevail,
To join your hearts in love and amity.
O, what a scandal is it to our crown,
That two such noble peers as ye should jar!
Believe me, lords, my tender years can tell
Civil dissension is a viperous worm
That gnaws the bowels of the commonwealth.
[A noise within, 'Down with the tawny-coats!']
What tumult's this?

WARWICK.
An uproar, I dare warrant,
Begun through malice of the bishop's men.

[A noise again, 'Stones! stones!' Enter Mayor.]

MAYOR.
O, my good lords, and virtuous Henry,
Pity the city of London, pity us!
The bishop and the Duke of Gloucester's men,
Forbidden late to carry any weapon,
Have fill'd their pockets full of pebble stones,
And banding themselves in contrary parts
Do pelt so fast at one another's pate
That many have their giddy brains knock'd out:
Our windows are broke down in every street,
And we for fear compell'd to shut our shops.

[Enter Serving-men, in skirmish, with bloody pates.]

KING.
We charge you, on allegiance to ourself,
To hold your slaughtering hands and keep the peace.
Pray, uncle Gloucester, mitigate this strife.

FIRST SERVING-MAN.
Nay, if we be forbidden stones,
we 'll fall to it with our teeth.

SECOND SERVING-MAN.
Do what ye dare, we are as resolute.

[Skirmish again.]

GLOUCESTER.
You of my household, leave this peevish broil

And set this unaccustom'd fight aside.

*do your scandalous opinions have to be discussed by the*
*Lords?"*
*Otherwise I would lay into Winchester.*

*Uncles of Gloucestershire and of Winchester,*
*these special guardians of our English kingdom,*
*I wish, if prayers are answered,*
*to join your hearts in love and friendship.*
*It's a great offence to my crown,*
*that to such noble peers as you should argue!*
*Believe me, lords, even at my young age I know*
*that civil disputes are a poisonous snake*
*that chew on the innards of the Commonwealth.*

*What's this racket?*

*A riot, I daresay,*
*started by the hatred of the Bishop's men.*

*Oh, my good lord, and good Henry,*
*pity the city of London, pity us!*
*The men of the Bishop and the Duke of Gloucester,*
*recently forbidden to carry any weapons,*
*have filled their pockets full of pebbles,*
*and grouping themselves into opposing gangs*
*are throwing them so hard at each other's heads*
*that many have had their stupid brains knocked out:*
*there are windows broken in every street,*
*and we have been forced to close the shops out of fear.*

*I order you, out of your loyalty to me,*
*to stop this slaughter and keep the peace.*
*Please, uncle Gloucester, end this disagreement.*

*No, if we are told we can't use stones,*
*we'll start fighting with our teeth.*

*Bring it on, we are as brave as you.*

*Those of you from my household, stop this childish*
*argument*
*and let's have no more of this unusual fighting.*

THIRD SERVING-MAN.
My lord, we know your grace to be a man
Just and upright; and, for your royal birth,
Inferior to none but to his Majesty:
And ere that we will suffer such a prince,
So kind a father of the commonweal,
To be disgraced by an inkhorn mate,
We and our wives and children all will fight,
And have our bodies slaughter'd by thy foes.

*My Lord, we know your grace is a just*
*and upright man; and, due to your royal birth,*
*you are inferior to nobody but his Majesty:*
*and before we will allow such a Prince,*
*such a great father to the country,*
*to be insulted by a lowborn clerk,*
*we and our wives and children will all fight,*
*and be slaughtered by your enemies.*

FIRST SERVING-MAN.
Aye, and the very parings of our nails
Shall pitch a field when we are dead.

*Yes, and when we are dead, our very*
*nail clippings can be used to build defences.*

[Begin again.]

GLOUCESTER.
Stay, stay, I say!
And if you love me, as you say you do,
Let me persuade you to forbear awhile.

*Stop, stop, I say!*
*If you love me as you claim you do,*
*do as I say and stop for a while.*

KING.
O, how this discord doth afflict my soul!
Can you, my Lord of Winchester, behold
My sighs and tears and will not once relent?
Who should be pitiful, if you be not?
Or who should study to prefer a peace,
If holy churchmen take delight in broils?

*Oh, how this fighting upsets my soul!*
*My Lord Winchester, can you look at*
*my sighs and tears and still not stop it?*
*Who will show pity, if not you?*
*Who will make any effort to keep the peace,*
*if holy churchmen enjoy fighting?*

WARWICK.
Yield, my lord protector; yield, Winchester;
Except you mean with obstinate repulse
To slay your sovereign and destroy the realm.
You see what mischief and what murder too
Hath been enacted through your enmity;
Then be at peace, except ye thirst for blood.

*Stop, my lord protector; stop, Winchester;*
*unless you mean with your obstinate refusal*
*to kill your King and destroy the kingdom.*
*You can see what mischief and what murder has*
*been caused by your opposition;*
*then be peaceful, unless you are desperate for bloodshed.*

WINCHESTER.
He shall submit, or I will never yield.

*He must obey, or I never will.*

GLOUCESTER.
Compassion on the king commands me stoop;
Or I would see his heart out, ere the priest
Should ever get that privilege of me.

*Compassion for the King makes me stop;*
*otherwise I would tear the heart out of*
*the priest, before I would surrender to him.*

WARWICK.
Behold, my Lord of Winchester, the duke
Hath banish'd moody discontented fury,
As by his smoothed brows it doth appear:
Why look you still so stern and tragical?

*See, my Lord of Winchester, the Duke*
*has dropped his moody unhappy fury,*
*as you can see by his unfurrowed brow:*
*why are you still looking so stern and tragic?*

GLOUCESTER.
Here, Winchester, I offer thee my hand.

*Here, Winchester, I offer you my hand.*

KING.
Fie, uncle Beaufort! I have heard you preach

*Come, uncle Beaufort! I have heard you preaching*

That malice was a great and grievous sin;
And will not you maintain the thing you teach,
But prove a chief offender in the same?

WARWICK.
Sweet king! the bishop hath a kindly gird.
For shame, my lord of Winchester, relent!
What, shall a child instruct you what to do?

WINCHESTER.
Well, Duke of Gloucester, I will yield to thee;
Love for thy love and hand for hand I give.

GLOUCESTER.
*[Aside]* Aye, but, I fear me, with a hollow heart.--
See here, my friends and loving countrymen;
This token serveth for a flag of truce
Betwixt ourselves and all our followers:
So help me God, as I dissemble not!

WINCHESTER.
*[Aside]* So help me God, as I intend it not!

KING.
O loving uncle, kind Duke of Gloucester,
How joyful am I made by this contract!
Away, my masters! trouble us no more;
But join in friendship, as your lords have done.

FIRST SERVING-MAN.
Content:  I'll to the surgeon's.

SECOND SERVING-MAN.
And so will I.

THIRD SERVING-MAN.
And I will see what physic the tavern affords.

*[Exeunt Serving-men, Mayor, &C.]*

WARWICK.
Accept this scroll, most gracious sovereign;
Which in the right of Richard Plantagenet
We do exhibit to your majesty.

GLOUCESTER.
Well urged, my Lord of Warwick: for, sweet prince,
An if your Grace mark every circumstance,
You have great reason to do Richard right:
Especially for those occasions
At Eltham place I told your majesty.

KING.
And those occasions, uncle, were of force;
Therefore, my loving lords, our pleasure is
That Richard be restored to his blood.

---

*that malice was a terrible sin;*
*will you not practice what you preach,*
*but show yourself one of the worst offenders?*

*Sweet King! That's the right way to reprove the Bishop.*
*My Lord Winchester, stop, for shame!*
*What, do you have to be told what to do by a child?*

*Well, Duke of Gloucester, I will give way to you;*
*I will exchange love for love and give hand for hand.*

*Yes, but I'm afraid it's not genuine.–*
*See here, my friends and loving countrymen;*
*this symbolises the start of a truce*
*between us and all our followers:*
*I swear to God I am genuine!*

*And I swear to God, I don't mean it!*

*O loving uncle, kind Duke of Gloucester,*
*how happy this agreement makes me!*
*Off you go, my lads! Don't give us any more trouble;*
*be friends, as your lords are.*

*I am satisfied: I shall go to the surgeon.*

*And so will I.*

*And I shall see what medicine there is in the pub.*

*Accept this document, most gracious king;*
*which I am showing your majesty*
*on behalf of Richard Plantagenet.*

*Well said, my Lord of Warwick: for, sweet prince,*
*if your Grace examines every part of the case,*
*you have every reason to do right by Richard:*
*especially for those reasons*
*I told your Majesty about at Eltham Palace.*

*And those reasons, uncle, were strong ones;*
*therefore, my loving lords, I have decided*
*that Richard should be given back his title.*

WARWICK.
Let Richard be restored to his blood;
So shall his father's wrongs be recompensed.

*Let Richard be given back his title;*
*and so the wrongs done to his father shall be paid for.*

WINCHESTER.
As will the rest, so willeth Winchester.

*Winchester agrees with what the others want.*

KING.
If Richard will be true, not that alone
But all the whole inheritance I give
That doth belong unto the house of York,
From whence you spring by lineal descent.

*If Richard will be loyal, I won't just give that back,*
*but the whole inheritance*
*which belongs to the house of York,*
*from which you are a direct descendant.*

PLANTAGENET.
Thy humble servant vows obedience
And humble service till the point of death.

*Your humble servant promises his obedience*
*and humble service until he dies.*

KING.
Stoop then and set your knee against my foot;
And, in reguerdon of that duty done,
I girt thee with the valiant sword of York:
Rise, Richard, like a true Plantagenet,
And rise created princely Duke of York.

*Then kneel and put your knee against my foot;*
*and, in reward for your duty,*
*I hang the brave sword of York upon you:*
*rise, Richard, like a true Plantagenet,*
*created the princely Duke of York.*

PLANTAGENET.
And so thrive Richard as thy foes may fall!
And as my duty springs, so perish they
That grudge one thought against your majesty!

*So may Richard thrive as your enemies fall!*
*And as I shall do my duty, anyone who has*
*a single grudging thought against your Majesty shall die!*

ALL.
Welcome, high prince, the mighty Duke of York!

*Welcome, high Prince, the mighty Duke of York!*

SOMERSET.
*[Aside]* Perish, base prince, ignoble Duke of York!

*Die, low Prince, lowdown Duke of York!*

GLOUCESTER.
Now will it best avail your majesty
To cross the seas and to be crown'd in France:
The presence of a king engenders love
Amongst his subjects and his loyal friends,
As it disanimates his enemies.

*Now the best thing for your Majesty will be*
*to cross the sea and be crowned in France:*
*the presence of a king creates love*
*amongst his subjects and his loyal friends,*
*and it is dispiriting for his enemies.*

KING.
When Gloucester says the word, King Henry goes;
For friendly counsel cuts off many foes.

*What Gloucester says, King Henry does;*
*friendly advice defeats many enemies.*

GLOUCESTER.
Your ships already are in readiness.

*Your ships are already prepared.*

*[Sennet. Flourish. Exeunt all but Exeter.]*

EXETER.
Aye, we may march in England or in France,
Not seeing what is likely to ensue.
This late dissension grown betwixt the peers
Burns under feigned ashes of forged love,

*Yes, we can march through England or France,*
*ignoring what is likely to happen.*
*This late disagreement between the peers*
*is still burning under the fake ashes of forged love,*

And will at last break out into a flame;
As fest'red members rot but by degree,
Till bones and flesh and sinews fall away,
So will this base and envious discord breed.
And now I fear that fatal prophecy
Which in the time of Henry named the fifth
Was in the mouth of every sucking babe;
That Henry born at Monmouth should win all

And Henry born at Windsor lose all:
Which is so plain, that Exeter doth wish
His days may finish ere that hapless time.

[Exit.]

and eventually it will break out into flame;
as infected limbs only rot by stages,
until the bones and flesh and muscles all fall off,
this is how this low and jealous disagreement will proceed.
And now am afraid the fatal prophecy will come true,
which every child knew at the time
of Henry the Fifth;
that Henry who was born at Monmouth would win everything,
and Henry born at Windsor would lose everything:
it's so obvious, that Exeter wishes
that he will be die before that unhappy time arrives.

## SCENE II. France. Before Rouen.

*[Enter La Pucelle disguised, with four Soldiers with sacks upon their backs.]*

PUCELLE.
These are the city gates, the gates of Rouen,
Through which our policy must make a breach:
Take heed, be wary how you place your words;
Talk like the vulgar sort of market men
That come to gather money for their corn.
If we have entrance, as I hope we shall,
And that we find the slothful watch but weak,
I 'll by a sign give notice to our friends,
That Charles the Dauphin may encounter them.

*These are the city gates, the gates of Rouen,*
*through which we must find a way by cunning:*
*listen, be careful what you say;*
*talk as if you were low down market men*
*come to get payment for their corn.*
*If we get in, as I hope we will,*
*and we find the lazy guards are small in number,*
*I shall alert our friends with a sign,*
*so that Charles the Dauphin can attack.*

FIRST SOLDIER.
Our sacks shall be a mean to sack the city,
And we be lords and rulers over Rouen;
Therefore we 'll knock. *[Knocks.]*

*Our sacks shall be our tools to sack the city,*
*and we shall be lords and rulers over Rouen;*
*so we shall knock.*

WATCH.
*[Within]* Qui est la?

*Who's there?*

PUCELLE.
Paysans, pauvres gens de France;
Poor market folks that come to sell their corn.

*Peasants, poor Frenchmen;*
*poor market folks who have come to sell their corn.*

WATCH.
Enter, go in; the market bell is rung.

*Come in; the market bell has been rung.*

PUCELLE.
Now, Rouen, I 'll shake thy bulwarks to the ground.
*[Exeunt.]*

*Now, Rouen, I'll shake your defences to the ground.*

*[Enter Charles, the Bastard of Orleans, Alencon, Reignier, and forces.]*

CHARLES.
Saint Denis bless this happy stratagem!
And once again we 'll sleep secure in Rouen.

*May Saint Denis bless this cunning plan!*
*Once again we'll sleep soundly in Rouen.*

BASTARD.
Here enter'd Pucelle and her practisants;
Now she is there, how will she specify
Here is the best and safest passage in?

*The Pucelle and her conspirators went in here;*
*now she's in, how will she let us know*
*that this is the best way to go?*

REIGNIER.
By thrusting out a torch from yonder tower;
Which, once discern'd, shows that her meaning is,
No way to that, for weakness, which she enter'd.

*She will hold up a torch from that tower;*
*once we see it we will know she's telling us*
*that the way she came in is the weakest point.*

*[Enter La Pucelle, on the top, thrusting out a torch burning.]*

PUCELLE.
Behold, this is the happy wedding torch
That joineth Rouen unto her countrymen,

*See, this is the happy wedding torch*
*that marries Rouen and her countrymen,*

But burning fatal to the Talbotites!

*but burns fatally for the Talbotites!*

[Exit.]

BASTARD.
See, noble Charles, the beacon of our friend;
The burning torch in yonder turret stands.

*See, noble Charles, the light of our friend;*
*the torch is burning on that tower.*

CHARLES.
Now shine it like a comet of revenge,
A prophet to the fall of all our foes!

*Let it shine like a revenging comet,*
*prophesying the fall of all our enemies!*

REIGNIER.
Defer no time, delays have dangerous ends;
Enter, and cry, 'The Dauphin!' presently,
And then do execution on the watch.

*Waste no time, delay could be fatal;*
*go in and give the shout of "The Dauphin!" at once,*
*and then destroy the guards.*

[Alarum. Exeunt.]

[An alarum. Enter Talbot in an excursion.]

TALBOT.
France, thou shalt rue this treason with thy tears,
If Talbot but survive thy treachery.
Pucelle, that witch, that damned sorceress,
Hath wrought this hellish mischief unawares,
That hardly we escaped the pride of France.

*France, you shall regret this treason with your tears,*
*if Talbot can just survive your treachery.*
*Pucelle, that witch, that dammed sorceress,*
*started this hellish mischief behind our backs,*
*so that we hardly escaped the nobility of France.*

[Exit.]

[An alarum: excursions.]
[Bedford, brought in sick in a chair. Enter Talbot and Burgundy without: within La Pucelle, Charles, Bastard, Alencon, and Reignier, on the walls.]

PUCELLE.
Good morrow, gallants! want ye corn for bread?

*Good morning, brave gentlemen! Do you want corn for bread?*

I think the Duke of Burgundy will fast
Before he 'll buy again at such a rate:
'Twas full of darnel: do you like the taste?

*I think the Duke of Burgundy will starve*
*before he'll buy at that price again:*
*it was full of grass: do you like the taste?*

BURGUNDY.
Scoff on, vile fiend and shameless courtezan!
I trust ere long to choke thee with thine own,
And make thee curse the harvest of that corn.

*Keep mocking, horrid devil and shameless whore!*
*I hope before long I'll be choking you with your own corn,*
*and I'll make you regret you ever started this business.*

CHARLES.
Your Grace may starve perhaps before that time.

*Perhaps your Grace will starve before that happens.*

BEDFORD.
O, let no words, but deeds, revenge this treason!

*Let's not revenge this treason with words, but with deeds!*

PUCELLE.
What will you do, good graybeard? break a lance,
And run a tilt at death within a chair?

*What are you going to do, good greybeard? Break a lance,*
*and try and out joust death from your saddle?*

TALBOT.
Foul fiend of France, and hag of all despite,
Encompass'd with thy lustful paramours!
Becomes it thee to taunt his valiant age,
And twit with cowardice a man half dead?
Damsel, I 'll have a bout with you again,
Or else let Talbot perish with this shame.

PUCELLE.
Are ye so hot? yet, Pucelle, hold thy peace;
If Talbot do but thunder, rain will follow.

*[The English party whisper together in council. ]*

God speed the parliament! who shall be the speaker?

TALBOT.
Dare ye come forth and meet us in the field?

PUCELLE.
Belike your lordship takes us then for fools,
To try if that our own be ours or no.

TALBOT.
I speak not to that railing Hecate,
But unto thee, Alencon, and the rest;
Will ye, like soldiers, come and fight it out?

ALENCON.
Signior, no.

TALBOT.
Signior, hang! base muleters of France!
Like peasant foot-boys do they keep the walls,
And dare not take up arms like gentlemen.

PUCELLE.
Away, captains! let 's get us from the walls;
For Talbot means no goodness by his looks.
God be wi' you, my lord! we came but to tell you
That we are here.

*[Exeunt from the walls.]*

TALBOT.
And there will we be too, ere it be long,
Or else reproach be Talbot's greatest fame!
Vow, Burgundy, by honor of thy house,
Prick'd on by public wrongs sustain'd in France,

Either to get the town again or die:
And I, as sure as English Henry lives,
And as his father here was conqueror,
As sure as in this late-betrayed town
Great Coeur-de-lion's heart was buried,
So sure I swear to get the town or die.

---

*Foul devil of France, and hag hated by all,
surrounded with your lustful lovers!
Is it your place to taunt brave old men,
and accuse a man who is half dead of cowardice?
Lady, I shall fight with you again,
or may Talbot die with this shame.*

*That passionate, are you? But, Pucelle, keep your peace;
if Talbot thunders, there will be rain later.*

*God bless this Parliament! Who's going to be the speaker?*

*Do you dare to come out and do battle with us?*

*It seems your lordship takes us for fools,
who would risk what they already have.*

*I'm not speaking to that ranting witch,
but to you, Alencon, and the rest;
will you come and fight it out like soldiers?*

*Sir, we will not.*

*Sir, be hanged! Lowdown peasants of France!
They hide behind the walls like lowborn pageboys,
and do not dare to go into battle like gentlemen.*

*Come away, captains! Let's get away from the walls;
from the look on Talbot's face he means us no good.
May God be with you, my lord! We only came to tell you
that we are here.*

*And we will be there too, before long,
otherwise let criticism be all Talbot receives!
Make a vow, Burgundy, on the honour of your family,
spurred on by the public insults you have been given in France,
either to recapture this town or die:
and I, as sure as English Henry is alive,
as his father was a conqueror here,
as sure as the heart of the great Richard
the Lionheart is buried in here,
I swear by all this I will capture the town or die.*

BURGUNDY.
My vows are equal partners with thy vows.

*My vows are equal to your own.*

TALBOT.
But, ere we go, regard this dying prince,

*But, before we go, we must pay attention to this dying Prince,*

The valiant Duke of Bedford. Come, my lord,
We will bestow you in some better place,
Fitter for sickness and for crazy age.

*the brave Duke of Bedford. Come, my lord,*
*we will put you in some better place,*
*more suitable for sickness and for fragile age.*

BEDFORD.
Lord Talbot, do not so dishonor me:
Here will I sit before the walls of Rouen,
And will be partner of your weal or woe.

*Lord Talbot, do not insult me like this:*
*I will sit here in front of the walls of Rouen,*
*and will be your partner in your wounds or sorrows.*

BURGUNDY.
Courageous Bedford, let us now persuade you.

*Brave Bedford, please let us persuade you.*

BEDFORD.
Not to be gone from hence; for once I read
That stout Pendragon in his litter sick
Came to the field and vanquished his foes.
Methinks I should revive the soldiers' hearts,
Because I ever found them as myself.

*Not to leave here; I once read*
*that great King Arthur was carried onto the battlefield when ill and beat his enemies.*
*I think I should stay here to give courage to the soldiers,*
*because I've always had a kinship with them.*

TALBOT.
Undaunted spirit in a dying breast!
Then be it so:  heavens keep old Bedford safe!
And now no more ado, brave Burgundy,
But gather we our forces out of hand
And set upon our boasting enemy.

*Brave spirit in a dying heart!*
*Then let it be so: may heaven keep old Bedford safe!*
*And now no more delay, brave Burgundy,*
*let's gather up our forces at once*
*and attack our arrogant enemy.*

*[Exeunt all but Bedford and Attendants.]*

*[An alarum:  excursions. Enter Sir John Fastolfe and a Captain.]*

CAPTAIN.
Whither away, Sir John Fastolfe, in such haste?

*Where are you going, Sir John Fastolfe, so quickly?*

FASTOLFE.
Whither away! to save myself by flight:
We are like to have the overthrow again.

*Where am I going! To save myself by running away:*
*we are probably going to be beaten again.*

CAPTAIN.
What! Will you fly, and leave Lord Talbot?

*What! Will you run, and leave Lord Talbot?*

FASTOLFE.
Aye,
All the Talbots in the world, to save my life.

*Yes,*
*all the Talbots in the world, to save my life.*

*[Exit.]*

CAPTAIN.
Cowardly knight! ill fortune follow thee!

*Cowardly knight! May bad luck follow you!*

*[Exit.]*

*[Retreat: excursions. La Pucelle, Alencon, and Charles fly.]*

BEDFORD.
Now, quiet soul, depart when heaven please,
For I have seen our enemies' overthrow.
What is the trust or strength of foolish man?
They that of late were daring with their scoffs
Are glad and fain by flight to save themselves.

*Now, quiet soul, you can leave when heaven orders,*
*for I have seen our enemies beaten.*
*What consistency or strength is there in foolish humanity?*
*Those who were recently talking so big*
*are now fleeing to save themselves.*

*[Bedford dies, and is carried in by two in his chair.]*

*[An alarum. Re-enter Talbot, Burgundy, and the rest.]*

TALBOT.
Lost, and recover'd in a day again!
This is a double honor, Burgundy:
Yet heavens have glory for this victory!

*Lost and recaptured in a day!*
*This is doubly honourable, Burgundy:*
*praise the heavens for this victory!*

BURGUNDY.
Warlike and martial Talbot, Burgundy
Enshrines thee in his heart, and there erects
Thy noble deeds as valor's monuments.

*Warlike and martial Talbot, Burgundy*
*venerates you in his heart, and places*
*your noble deeds there as monuments to bravery.*

TALBOT.
Thanks, gentle duke. But where is Pucelle now?
I think her old familiar is asleep:
Now where 's the Bastard's braves, and Charles his
gleeks?
What, all amort? Rouen hangs her head for grief
That such a valiant company are fled.
Now will we take some order in the town,
Placing therein some expert officers;
And then depart to Paris to the king,
For there young Henry with his nobles lie.

*Thanks, gentle Duke. But where is Pucelle now?*
*I think her spiritual accomplice is asleep:*
*now where are the Bastard's challenges, and the jokes of*
*Charles?*
*What, all dead? Rouen hangs her head in grief*
*that such a brave company has fled.*
*Now we will establish order in the town,*
*placing some expert officers in charge;*
*and then we shall go to Paris to see the King,*
*for that is where young Henry and his noblemen are.*

BURGUNDY.
What wills Lord Talbot pleaseth Burgundy.

*What Lord Talbot wants is pleasing to Burgundy.*

TALBOT.
But yet, before we go, let 's not forget
The noble Duke of Bedford late deceased,
But see his exequies fulfill'd in Rouen:
A braver soldier never couched lance,
A gentler heart did never sway in court;
But kings and mightiest potentates must die,
For that's the end of human misery.

*But still, before we go, let's not forget*
*the recently deceased Duke of Bedford,*
*and make sure his funeral rites are done in Rouen:*
*a braver soldier never held a lance,*
*and a more gentle heart never ruled a court;*
*but Kings and the greatest of rulers must die,*
*for that is the way we end the misery of life.*

*[Exeunt.]*

# SCENE III. The plains near Rouen.

*[Enter Charles, the Bastard of Orleans, Alencon, La Pucelle, and forces.]*

PUCELLE.
Dismay not, princes, at this accident,
Nor grieve that Rouen is so recovered:
Care is no cure, but rather corrosive,
For things that are not to be remedied.
Let frantic Talbot triumph for a while
And like a peacock sweep along his tail;
We 'll pull his plumes and take away his train,
If Dauphin and the rest will be but ruled.

*Do not be dismayed, Princes, at this unlucky event,*
*nor grieve that Rouen has been recaptured:*
*there's no sense in worrying about*
*things we can do nothing about.*
*Let mad Talbot enjoy his triumph for a while,*
*and flaunt his tail like a peacock;*
*we'll pull out his feathers and remove his tail,*
*if the Dauphin and his followers will do as I say.*

CHARLES.
We have been guided by thee hitherto,
And of thy cunning had no diffidence:
One sudden foil shall never breed distrust.

*We have been guided by you so far,*
*and had no doubts about your plans:*
*one setback won't unsettle our faith.*

BASTARD.
Search out thy wit for secret policies,
And we will make thee famous through the world.

*Use your intelligence to devise cunning plans,*
*and we will make you famous throughout the world.*

ALENCON.
We'll set thy statue in some holy place,
And have thee reverenced like a blessed saint.
Employ thee then, sweet virgin, for our good.

*We'll put up your statue in some holy place,*
*and have you worshipped like a blessed saint.*
*Get to work then, sweet virgin, for our good.*

PUCELLE.
Then thus it must be; this doth Joan devise:
By fair persuasions mix'd with sugar'd words
We will entice the Duke of Burgundy
To leave the Talbot and to follow us.

*Then this is how it must be; this is what Joan advises:*
*with good offers mixed with sweet words*
*we shall persuade the Duke of Burgundy*
*to leave Talbot and follow us.*

CHARLES.
Aye, marry, sweeting, if we could do that,
France were no place for Henry's warriors;
Nor should that nation boast it so with us,
But be extirped from our provinces.

*Well, yes, sweetheart, if we could do that,*
*France would be no place for Henry's soldiers;*
*that country wouldn't keep up the fight with us,*
*they would be thrown out of our lands.*

ALENCON.
For ever should they be expulsed from France,
And not have title of an earldom here.

*They would be expelled from France forever,*
*and they would not have so much as an earldom left here.*

PUCELLE.
Your honours shall perceive how I will work
To bring this matter to the wished end.

*Your Honours will see how I work*
*to bring this matter to its desired conclusion.*

*[Drum sounds afar off.]*

Hark! by the sound of drum you may perceive
Their powers are marching unto Paris-ward.
Here sound an English march. Enter, and pass over

at a distance, Talbot and his forces.

*Listen—by the sound of the drum you can hear that*
*their forces are marching to Paris.*
*Hear the sound of the English marching: entering and*
*passing by*
*At a distance, Talbot and his Army*

There goes the Talbot, with his colors spread,
And all the troops of English after him.

*[French march. Enter the Duke of Burgundy and forces.]*

Now in the rearward comes the duke and his:
Fortune in favor makes him lag behind.
Summon a parley; we will talk with him.

*[Trumpets sound a parley.]*

CHARLES.
A parley with the Duke of Burgundy!

BURGUNDY.
Who craves a parley with the Burgundy?

PUCELLE.
The princely Charles of France, thy countryman.

BURGUNDY.
What say'st thou, Charles? for I am marching hence.

CHARLES.
Speak, Pucelle, and enchant him with thy words.

PUCELLE.
Brave Burgundy, undoubted hope of France!
Stay, let thy humble handmaid speak to thee.

BURGUNDY.
Speak on; but be not over-tedious.

PUCELLE.
Look on thy country, look on fertile France,
And see the cities and the towns defaced
By wasting ruin of the cruel foe.
As looks the mother on her lowly babe
When death doth close his tender dying eyes,
See, see the pining malady of France;
Behold the wounds, the most unnatural wounds,
Which thou thyself hast given her woful breast.
O, turn thy edged sword another way;
Strike those that hurt, and hurt not those that help.

One drop of blood drawn from thy country's bosom
Should grieve thee more than streams of foreign gore:
Return thee therefore with a flood of tears,
And wash away thy country's stained spots.

BURGUNDY.
Either she hath bewitch'd me with her words,
Or nature makes me suddenly relent.

PUCELLE.
Besides, all French and France exclaims on thee,

---

*There goes Talbot with his banners flying,
and all the English forces following him.*

*Now behind him comes the Duke and his:
fortune favours us, making him fall behind.
Call a meeting. We shall talk to him.*

*We wish to speak with the Duke of Burgundy!*

*Who wants to speak with the Duke of Burgundy?*

*The royal Charles of France, your countryman.*

*What you have to say, Charles? I'm marching away.*

*Speak, Pucelle, and enchant him with your words.*

*Brave Burgundy, the greatest hope in France!
Wait, let your humble servant speak to you.*

*Speak, but don't drag it out.*

*Look at your country, look at fertile France,
see the cities and towns damaged
by the vicious attacks of the cruel enemy.
As a mother looks on her tiny baby
when death closes his sweet dying eyes,
see the terrible illness of France;
see the wounds, the most unnatural wounds,
which you yourself have inflicted on her.
Oh, turn your sharp sword in another direction;
attack those who are wounding, don't wound those who
help you.*

*One drop of blood from your countrymen should give you
more grief than rivers of foreign blood:
so come back with a flood of tears,
and wash away the bloodstains on your country.*

*Either she has bewitched me with her words,
or nature has suddenly made me change my mind.*

*Besides, all of France and the French cry out against you,*

Doubting thy birth and lawful progeny.
Who join'st thou with but with a lordly nation
That will not trust thee but for profit's sake?
When Talbot hath set footing once in France,
And fashion'd thee that instrument of ill,
Who then but English Henry will be lord,
And thou be thrust out like a fugitive?
Call we to mind, and mark but this for proof,
Was not the Duke of Orleans thy foe?
And was he not in England prisoner?
But when they heard he was thine enemy,
They set him free without his ransom paid,
In spite of Burgundy and all his friends.
See, then, thou fight'st against thy countrymen
And join'st with them will be thy slaughtermen.
Come, come, return; return, thou wandering lord;
Charles and the rest will take thee in their arms.

BURGUNDY.
I am vanquished; these haughty words of hers
Have batt'red me like roaring cannon-shot,
And made me almost yield upon my knees.
Forgive me, country, and sweet countrymen,
And, lords, accept this hearty kind embrace:
My forces and my power of men are yours:
So, farewell, Talbot; I 'll no longer trust thee.

PUCELLE.
[Aside] Done like a Frenchman: turn and turn again!

CHARLES.
Welcome, brave duke; thy friendship makes us fresh.

BASTARD.
And doth beget new courage in our breasts.

ALENCON.
Pucelle hath bravely play'd her part in this,
And doth deserve a coronet of gold.

CHARLES.
Now let us on, my lords, and join our powers,
And seek how we may prejudice the foe.

*[Exeunt.]*

*doubting your birth and legitimacy.*
*Who are you allied to but a haughty nation,*
*who will only use you for their own profit?*
*When Talbot has got a foothold here in France,*
*using you to achieve that evil end,*
*who but English Henry will rule?*
*You will be thrown out like a fugitive.*
*Let's remember–just think of this–*
*wasn't the Duke of Orleans your enemy?*
*And wasn't he prisoner in England?*
*But when they heard he was your enemy*
*they set him free without asking for a ransom,*
*to spite Burgundy and his allies.*
*So you see, you are fighting your own countrymen,*
*and on the side of those who would like to kill you.*
*Come, come, come back; come back, you wandering lord.*
*Charles and the others will welcome you.*

*I have been beaten; these proud words of hers*
*have battered me like shot from a cannon,*
*and made me surrender, almost down on my knees.*
*Forgive me, my country, and sweet countrymen,*
*and lords, except this happy sincere embrace:*
*my men and I are at your service:*
*so, farewell, Talbot; I shall no longer trust you.*

*Done like a Frenchman: always changing sides!*

*Welcome, brave Duke; your friendship rejuvenates us.*

*You've put new courage into our hearts.*

*Pucelle has done her part well in this,*
*and deserves a golden crown.*

*Now let's go on, my lords, and join our forces,*
*and see what harm we can do our enemies.*

## SCENE IV. Paris. The palace.

[Enter the King, Gloucester, Bishop of Winchester, York, Suffolk, Somerset, Warwick, Exeter: Vernon, Basset, and others. To them with his soldiers, Talbot.]

TALBOT.
My gracious Prince, and honourable peers,
Hearing of your arrival in this realm,
I have awhile given truce unto my wars,
To do my duty to my sovereign:
In sign whereof, this arm, that hath reclaim'd
To your obedience fifty fortresses,
Twelve cities and seven walled towns of strength,
Beside five hundred prisoners of esteem,
Lets fall his sword before your highness' feet,
And with submissive loyalty of heart
Ascribes the glory of his conquest got
First to my God and next unto your grace. [Kneels.]

*My gracious Prince, and honourable peers,*
*hearing of your arrival in this country,*
*I have suspended my military activities for a while,*
*to pay my respects to my Monarch:*
*as a symbol of this, this arm, that has captured*
*for your Highness fifty fortresses,*
*twelve cities and seven strong walled towns,*
*as well as five hundred noble prisoners,*
*lays his sword at the feet of your Highness,*
*and with a humble loyal heart*
*attributes the glory of his victories*
*firstly to God, and next to your Grace.*

KING.
Is this the Lord Talbot, uncle Gloucester,
That hath so long been resident in France?

*Uncle Gloucester, is this the Lord Talbot,*
*who has been living in France for so long?*

GLOUCESTER.
Yes, if it please your majesty, my liege.

*It is, my lord.*

KING.
Welcome, brave captain and victorious lord!
When I was young, as yet I am not old,
I do remember how my father said
A stouter champion never handled sword.
Long since we were resolved of your truth,
Your faithful service and your toil in war;
Yet never have you tasted our reward,
Or been reguerdon'd with so much as thanks,
Because till now we never saw your face:
Therefore, stand up: and for these good deserts,
We here create you Earl of Shrewsbury;
And in our coronation take your place.

*Welcome, brave captain and victorious lord!*
*When I was young—I'm still not old—*
*I can remember my father saying*
*that no braver man ever handled a sword.*
*For a long time I have known of your loyalty,*
*your faithful service and your military efforts;*
*but you have never been rewarded by me,*
*or even received my thanks in compensation,*
*because until now I had never met you:*
*so, stand up: for all your good efforts,*
*I declare you the Earl of Shrewsbury;*
*you shall take your place at my coronation.*

[Sennet. Flourish. Exeunt all but Vernon and Basset.]

VERNON.
Now, sir, to you, that were so hot at sea,
Disgracing of these colors that I wear
In honor of my noble Lord of York:--
Dar'st thou maintain the former words thou spakest?

*Now, sir, you who were so brave on board ship,*
*insulting these colours that I wear*
*in honour of my noble Lord of York:*
*do you stick by what you said before?*

BASSET.
Yes, sir; as well as you dare patronage
The envious barking of your saucy tongue
Against my lord the Duke of Somerset.

*Yes sir, just as much as you carry on*
*with your cheeky insults against*
*my lord the Duke of Somerset.*

VERNON.
Sirrah, thy lord I honor as he is.

*Sir, I honour your lord for what he is.*

BASSET.
Why, what is he? as good a man as York.

*Why, what is he? He's as good a man as York.*

VERNON.
Hark ye; not so: in witness, take ye that.

*You listen, that's not true: to show you that, take that.*

*[Strikes him.]*

BASSET.
Villain, thou know'st the law of arms is such
That whoso draws a sword, 'tis present death,
Or else this blow should broach thy dearest blood.

But I 'll unto his majesty, and crave
I may have liberty to venge this wrong;
When thou shalt see I 'll meet thee to thy cost.

*Villain, you know that military law is such
that whoever draws a sword will be executed at once,
or otherwise your blood would be spilt in return for this
blow.
But I shall go to his Majesty, and beg him
to give me permission to take my revenge for this insult;
then you'll see I will fight you to your cost.*

VERNON.
Well, miscreant, I 'll be there as soon as you;
And, after, meet you sooner than you would.

*Well, you scoundrel, I'll get there at the same time as you;
and after that I'll be more willing to fight a duel than you.*

*[Exeunt.]*

# Act IV

## SCENE I. Paris. A hall of state.

*[Enter the King, Gloucester, Bishop of Winchester, York, Suffolk, Somerset, Warwick, Talbot, Exeter, the Governor of Paris, and others.]*

GLOUCESTER.
Lord bishop, set the crown upon his head.

*Lord Bishop, put the crown on his head.*

WINCHESTER.
God save King Henry, of that name the sixth!

*God save King Henry, the sixth of that name!*

GLOUCESTER.
Now, Governor of Paris, take your oath,
That you elect no other king but him;
Esteem none friends but such as are his friends,
And none your foes but such as shall pretend
Malicious practices against his state:
This shall ye do, so help you righteous God!

*Now, Governor of Paris, take your oath,
that you will choose no other king but him;
that you will not count anybody as allies except his allies,
and that your only enemies will be those
who undertake malicious actions against his position:
swear you shall do this, so help you righteous God!*

*[Enter Sir John Fastolfe.]*

FASTOLFE.
My gracious sovereign, as I rode from Calais,
To haste unto your coronation,
A letter was deliver'd to my hands,
Writ to your Grace from the Duke of Burgundy.

*My gracious sovereign, as I rode from Calais,
hurrying to your coronation,
a letter was put into my hands,
written to your grace from the Duke of Burgundy.*

TALBOT.
Shame to the Duke of Burgundy and thee!
I vow'd, base knight, when I did meet thee next,
To tear the garter from thy craven's leg,
*[Plucking it off.]*
Which I have done, because unworthily
Thou wast installed in that high degree.
Pardon me, princely Henry, and the rest:
This dastard, at the battle of Patay,
When but in all I was six thousand strong
And that the French were almost ten to one,
Before we met or that a stroke was given,
Like to a trusty squire did run away:
In which assault we lost twelve hundred men;
Myself and divers gentlemen beside
Were there surprised and taken prisoners.
Then judge, great lords, if I have done amiss;
Or whether that such cowards ought to wear
This ornament of knighthood, yea or no.

*Shame on the Duke of Burgundy and on you!
I swore, degraded knight, that the next time I saw you
I would tear the garter off your coward's leg,*

*which I have done, because you did not deserve
to be given that great honour.
Excuse me, princely Henry, and you others:
this bastard, at the battle of Poitiers,
when I only had six thousand men
and the French outnumbered us almost ten to one,
before we met or any blows were struck,
he ran away like a complete coward:
in that battle we lost twelve hundred men;
myself and other gentlemen besides
were ambushed there and taken prisoner.
So judge, great lords, if I have done anything wrong;
or whether cowards like him should be allowed to wear
this badge of knighthood, yes or no.*

GLOUCESTER.
To say the truth, this fact was infamous
And ill beseeming any common man,
Much more a knight, a captain, and a leader.

*To tell the truth, this matter was notorious
and it would look bad for any common man,
let alone a knight, a captain, and a leader.*

TALBOT.
When first this order was ordain'd, my lords,
Knights of the garter were of noble birth,
Valiant and virtuous, full of haughty courage,
Such as were grown to credit by the wars;
Not fearing death, nor shrinking for distress,
But always resolute in most extremes.
He then that is not furnish'd in this sort
Doth but usurp the sacred name of knight,
Profaning this most honorable order,
And should, if I were worthy to be judge,
Be quite degraded, like a hedge-born swain
That doth presume to boast of gentle blood.

KING.
Stain to thy countrymen, thou hear'st thy doom!
Be packing, therefore, thou that wast a knight;
Henceforth we banish thee, on pain of death.

[Exit Fastolfe.]

And now, my lord protector, view the letter
Sent from our uncle Duke of Burgundy.

GLOUCESTER.
What means his grace,
that he hath changed his style?
No more but, plain and bluntly, 'To the King!'
Hath he forgot he is his sovereign?
Or doth this churlish superscription
Pretend some alteration in good will?
What's here? [Reads] 'I have, upon especial cause,
Moved with compassion of my country's wreck,
Together with the pitiful complaints
Of such as your oppression feeds upon,
Forsaken your pernicious faction,
And join'd with Charles, the rightful King of France.'
O monstrous treachery! can this be so,
That in alliance, amity and oaths,
There should be found such false dissembling guile?

KING.
What! doth my uncle Burgundy revolt?

GLOUCESTER.
He doth, my lord, and is become your foe.

KING.
Is that the worst this letter doth contain?

GLOUCESTER.
It is the worst, and all, my lord, he writes.

KING.
Why, then, Lord Talbot there shall talk with him,
And give him chastisement for this abuse.

*When this order was first established, my lords,*
*Knights of the Garter were men of noble birth,*
*brave and good, full of proud courage,*
*the sort of people who got credit in war;*
*they did not fear death, nor facing danger,*
*but remained steadfast in the most desperate situations.*
*So somebody who does not have that sort of character*
*is just stealing the sacred name of knight,*
*dishonouring this most honourable order,*
*and he should, if I'm allowed to judge,*
*be quite humiliated, like a country peasant*
*who tries to boast that he has noble blood.*

*You blot on your countrymen, you've heard your sentence!*
*So get packing, you who were a knight;*
*I banish you from this place, on pain of death.*

*And now, my lord protector, let's see the letter*
*that our uncle the Duke of Burgundy sent.*

*What does his grace mean,*
*by changing his style like this?*
*He just says plainly and bluntly, "To the King!"*
*Has he forgotten who is his ruler?*
*Or does this curmudgeonly address*
*indicate some change in his attitude?*
*What's here? "I have, for special reasons,*
*moved by compassion at the destruction of my country,*
*and the pitiful suffering*
*of those whom you oppress,*
*left your evil party,*
*and joined with Charles, the true king of France."*
*O monstrous treachery! Can this really be happening,*
*that such false lying trickery could be found*
*amongst all the alliances, friendship and oaths?*

*What! Is my uncle Burgundy rebelling?*

*He is, my lord, and has become your enemy.*

*Is that the worst news in the letter?*

*It is the worst, my lord, in fact it's all he says.*

*Well, then, Lord Talbot shall speak with him,*
*and punish him for his crime.*

How say you, my lord? are you not content?

*What do you say, my lord? Are you happy with that?*

TALBOT.
Content, my liege! yes; but that I am prevented,
I should have begg'd I might have been employ'd.

*Happy, my lord! Yes; if it hadn't been bad etiquette,
I would have begged to be given this job.*

KING.
Then gather strength, and march unto him straight:
Let him perceive how ill we brook his treason,
And what offence it is to flout his friends.

*Then summon your forces, and march straight to him:
show him what we think of his treason,
and what a crime it is to insult his friends.*

TALBOT.
I go, my lord, in heart desiring still
You may behold confusion of your foes.

*I shall go, my lord, my heart's desire still being
you shall see your enemies defeated.*

[Exit.]

[Enter Vernon and Basset.]

VERNON.
Grant me the combat, gracious sovereign.

*Permit me to fight a duel, gracious sovereign.*

BASSET.
And me, my lord, grant me the combat too.

*And me, my lord, give me permission too.*

YORK.
This is my servant: hear him, noble prince.

*This is my servant: hear him, noble Prince.*

SOMERSET.
And this is mine: sweet Henry, favor him.

*And this is mine: sweet Henry, listen to him.*

KING.
Be patient, lords, and give them leave to speak.
Say, gentlemen, what makes you thus exclaim?
And wherefore crave you combat? or with whom?

*Calm down, lords, and give them a chance to speak.
Tell me, gentlemen, what got you so passionate?
Why do you want to fight a duel? And who with?*

VERNON.
With him, my lord; for he hath done me wrong.

*With him, my lord; for he has insulted me.*

BASSET.
And I with him; for he hath done me wrong.

*And I want to fight him; for he has insulted me.*

KING.
What is that wrong whereof you both complain?
First let me know, and then I'll answer you.

*What is this insult which you are both complaining of?
first tell me, and then I'll answer you.*

BASSET.
Crossing the sea from England into France,
This fellow here, with envious carping tongue,
Upbraided me about the rose I wear;
Saying, the sanguine colour of the leaves
Did represent my master's blushing cheeks,
When stubbornly he did repugn the truth
About a certain question in the law
Argued betwixt the Duke of York and him;
With other vile and ignominious terms:

*Crossing the sea from England to France,
this fellow here, with his jealous sniping tongue,
made fun of me for the rose I wear;
he said that the red colour of the leaves
represented the blushing cheeks of my master,
when he stubbornly refuted the truth
about a question of law that he was
arguing with the Duke of York;
he used other rude and disgraceful language:*

In confutation of which rude reproach,
And in defence of my lord's worthiness,
I crave the benefit of law of arms.

VERNON.
And that is my petition, noble lord:
For though he seem with forged quaint conceit
To set a gloss upon his bold intent,
Yet know, my lord, I was provoked by him;
And he first took exceptions at this badge,
Pronouncing that the paleness of this flower
Bewray'd the faintness of my master's heart.

YORK.
Will not this malice, Somerset, be left?

SOMERSET.
Your private grudge, my Lord of York, will out,
Though ne'er so cunningly you smother it.

KING.
Good Lord, what madness rules in brainsick men,
When for so slight and frivolous a cause
Such factious emulations shall arise!
Good cousins both, of York and Somerset,
Quiet yourselves, I pray, and be at peace.

YORK.
Let this dissension first be tried by fight,
And then your highness shall command a peace.

SOMERSET.
The quarrel toucheth none but us alone;
Betwixt ourselves let us decide it then.

YORK.
There is my pledge; accept it, Somerset.

VERNON.
Nay, let it rest where it began at first.

BASSET.
Confirm it so, mine honorable lord.

GLOUCESTER.
Confirm it so! Confounded be your strife!
And perish ye, with your audacious prate!
Presumptuous vassals, are you not ashamed
With this immodest clamorous outrage
To trouble and disturb the king and us?
And you, my lords, methinks you do not well
To bear with their perverse objections;
Much less to take occasion from their mouths
To raise a mutiny betwixt yourselves:
Let me persuade you take a better course.

in order to pay him back for his rudeness,
and to defend the reputation of my lord,
I begged to be allowed a duel.

That is what I ask also, noble lord:
for although he has made up a nice story
to cover up his transgression,
you should know, my lord, that I was provoked by him;
he was the first one to mock my badge,
saying that the paleness of this flower
represented the faintness of my master's heart.

Can't you drop this argument, Somerset?

Your secret grudge, my Lord of York, always appears,
however cunningly you try to hide it.

Good Lord, what madness is ruling you foolish men,
when for such a small and trivial reason
you start such great arguments!
My good cousins, York and Somerset,
calm down, please, and be at peace.

Let this argument be tested in combat first,
and then your Highness can order peace.

This quarrel affects nobody but ourselves;
let us decide it between us.

There is my challenge; accept it, Somerset.

No, let it stay where it first began.

Say you will, my honourable lord.

Say I will! Be damned to your arguments!
May you die, with your arrogant chatter!
You presumptuous servants, aren't you ashamed
to trouble and disturb the King and us
with these rude noisy outbursts?
And you, my lords, I don't think it's right
for you to support their stupid quarrel;
even less so to use their argument
to start a fight between yourselves:
let me persuade you of a better way of doing things.

EXETER.
It grieves his highness:  good my lords, be friends.

*You're upsetting his Highness: my good lords, be friends.*

KING.
Come hither, you that would be combatants:
Henceforth I charge you, as you love our favor,
Quite to forget this quarrel and the cause.
And you, my lords, remember where we are:
In France, amongst a fickle wavering nation;
If they perceive dissension in our looks
And that within ourselves we disagree,
How will their grudging stomachs be provoked
To willful disobedience, and rebel!
Beside, what infamy will there arise
When foreign princes shall be certified
That for a toy, a thing of no regard,
King Henry's peers and chief nobility
Destroy'd themselves and lost the realm of France
O, think upon the conquest of my father,
My tender years; and let us not forgo
That for a trifle that was bought with blood!
Let me be umpire in this doubtful strife.
I see no reason, if I wear this rose,
[Putting on a red rose.]
That any one should therefore be suspicious
I more incline to Somerset than York:
Both are my kinsmen, and I love them both:
As well they may upbraid me with my crown,
Because, forsooth, the king of Scots is crown'd.
But your discretions better can persuade
Than I am able to instruct or teach;
And, therefore, as we hither came in peace,
So let us still continue peace and love.
Cousin of York, we institute your grace
To be our Regent in these parts of France:
And, good my Lord of Somerset, unite
Your troops of horsemen with his bands of foot;
And, like true subjects, sons of your progenitors,
Go cheerfully together and digest
Your angry choler on your enemies.
Ourself, my lord protector and the rest
After some respite will return to Calais;
From thence to England; where I hope ere long
To be presented, by your victories,
With Charles, Alencon, and that traitorous rout.

*Come here, you who want to fight.*
*From now on I order you, if you want to serve me,*
*to completely forget this quarrel and the reasons for it.*
*And you, my lord; remember where we are—*
*in France, which is a fickle and changeable country.*
*If they see that we are arguing,*
*and that we have disagreements amongst ourselves,*
*how much that will provoke their disgruntled spirits*
*to be wilfully disobedient and rebel!*
*Besides, what a bad reputation we will get,*
*when foreign princes are notified that*
*for a trifle, something of no importance,*
*King Henry's peers and his greatest noblemen*
*destroyed themselves and lost France!*
*Think of the victory of my father,*
*my youth, and do not let us lose something*
*that we paid for with blood over a trifle.*
*Let me be the decider of this doubtful dispute*
*I see no reason, if I wear this rose,*
*[Takes the red rose from Basset]*
*for anybody to think*
*that I am more favourable to Somerset than York:*
*they are both kinsmen of mine, and I love them both.*
*Someone might as well criticise my having a crown*
*because the king of Scotland has one also.*
*But you can see the difference better*
*than I can teach it to you:*
*and so, as we came here in peace,*
*let us continue with peace and love.*
*My cousin York, I choose your Grace*
*to be my regent in these parts of France:*
*and you, my good lord of Somerset, I want you*
*to join your cavalry with his infantry,*
*and like true subjects, sons of your ancestors,*
*go out together happily and take out*
*your anger on your enemies.*
*I, my lord protector and the rest,*
*will after a little rest return to Calais,*
*and from there go to England—where I hope to see*
*before long, due to your victories,*
*Charles, Alencon and all that traitorous rabble.*

[Flourish. Exeunt all but York, Warwick, Exeter and  Vernon.]

WARWICK.
My Lord of York, I promise you, the king
Prettily, methought, did play the orator.

*My Lord of York, I tell you truly, I thought*
*the King spoke very well there.*

YORK.
And so he did; but yet I like it not,
In that he wears the badge of Somerset.

*He certainly did; but I don't like the fact*
*that he is wearing the badge of Somerset.*

WARWICK.
Tush, that was but his fancy, blame him not;
I dare presume, sweet prince, he thought no harm.

*Come now, that was just an example, don't blame him;*
*I daresay the sweet prince meant no harm.*

YORK.
An if I wist he did,--but let it rest;
Other affairs must now be managed.

*If I thought he did—but let it go;*
*there is other business on hand now.*

*[Exeunt all but Exeter.]*

EXETER.
Well didst thou, Richard, to suppress thy voice;
For, had the passions of thy heart burst out,
I fear we should have seen decipher'd there
More rancorous spite, more furious raging broils,
Than yet can be imagined or supposed.
But howsoe'er, no simple man that sees
This jarring discord of nobility,
This shouldering of each other in the court,
This factious bandying of their favorites,
But that it doth presage some ill event.
Tis much when scepters are in children's hands;
But more when envy breeds unkind division;
There comes the ruin, there begins confusion.

*You did well, Richard, not to speak out;*
*for if you had let what was in your heart escape,*
*I feel we should have seen revealed there*
*more angry spite, more furious arguments,*
*than anyone can presently imagine.*
*However that may be, no straightforward man who sees*
*these noblemen clashing with each other,*
*shouldering each other aside in the court,*
*these rows between their favourites,*
*could doubt that it foretells some unpleasant events.*
*It's dangerous when children have control of the sceptre;*
*more so when jealousy breeds aggressive divisions;*
*then ruin and chaos are not far away.*

*[Exit.]*

# SCENE II. Before Bordeaux.

*[Enter Talbot, with trump and drum.]*

TALBOT.
Go to the gates of Bordeaux, trumpeter:
Summon their general unto the wall.

*Go to the gates of Bordeaux, trumpeter:*
*call their general to the battlements.*

*[Trumpet sounds. Enter General and others, aloft.]*

English John Talbot, Captains, calls you forth,
Servant in arms to Harry King of England;
And thus he would: Open your city-gates,
Be humble to us; call my sovereign yours,
And do him homage as obedient subjects;
And I 'll withdraw me and my bloody power:
But, if you frown upon this proffer'd peace,
You tempt the fury of my three attendants,

Lean famine, quartering steel, and climbing fire;
Who in a moment even with the earth
Shall lay your stately and air-braving towers,
If you forsake the offer of their love.

*English John Talbot, captains, summons you out,*
*a military servant of Harry the King of England;*
*he demands this: open your city gates,*
*bow down to us; call my King yours,*
*and pay homage to him as obedient subjects;*
*then I shall withdraw myself and all my forces:*
*but, if you refuse this offer of peace,*
*you are exposing yourself to the anger of my three*
*assistants,*
*lean famine, slashing steel, and climbing fire;*
*in a moment they can bring your great towers*
*down to the level of the earth,*
*if you reject this offer of friendship.*

GENERAL.
Thou ominous and fearful owl of death,
Our nation's terror and their bloody scourge!
The period of thy tyranny approacheth.
On us thou canst not enter but by death;
For, I protest, we are well fortified
And strong enough to issue out and fight:
If thou retire, the Dauphin, well appointed,
Stands with the snares of war to tangle thee:
On either hand thee there are squadrons pitch'd
To wall thee from the liberty of flight;
And no way canst thou turn thee for redress,
But death doth front thee with apparent spoil,
And pale destruction meets thee in the face.
Ten thousand French have ta'en the sacrament
To rive their dangerous artillery
Upon no Christian soul but English Talbot.
Lo, there thou stand'st, a breathing valiant man,
Of an invincible unconquer'd spirit!
This is the latest glory of thy praise
That I, thy enemy, due thee withal;
For ere the glass, that now begins to run,
Finish the process of his sandy hour,
These eyes, that see thee now well colored,
Shall see thee wither'd, bloody, pale, and dead.

*You ominous and terrifying harbinger of death,*
*the terror of our nation and its bloody destroyer,*
*the end of your tyranny is coming.*
*You cannot come in here except by killing us:*
*for I tell you that we are well defended*
*and strong enough to come out and fight.*
*If you retreat, the Dauphin is waiting, well equipped*
*with the nets of war to catch you.*
*On either side of you there are squadrons lined up*
*to keep you from escaping;*
*there is no way you can turn for help,*
*death is confronting you with visible ruin,*
*and pale destruction is staring you in the face.*
*Ten thousand Frenchmen have sworn by the sacrament*
*to fire their dangerous artillery*
*on no Christian soul apart from English Talbot.*
*Look, there you stand a brave live man*
*with an invincible unconquered spirit:*
*this is the last praise you will receive,*
*and I, your enemy, give it to you as your due:*
*for now the hourglass has been started running,*
*and at the end of its time*
*these eyes which now see you healthy*
*shall see you withered, bloody, pale and dead.*

*[Drum afar off.]*

Hark! hark! the Dauphin's drum, a warning bell,
Sings heavy music to thy timorous soul;

*Listen, listen; the Dauphin's drum, it sounds a warning,*
*heavy music for your fearful soul,*

And mine shall ring thy dire departure out.

*[Exeunt General, etc.]*

TALBOT.
He fables not; I hear the enemy:
Out, some light horsemen, and peruse their wings.

O, negligent and heedless discipline!
How are we park'd and bounded in a pale,
A little herd of England's timorous deer,
Mazed with a yelping kennel of French curs!
If we be English deer, be then in blood;
Not rascal-like, to fall down with a pinch,
But rather, moody-mad and desperate stags,
Turn on the bloody hounds with heads of steel
And make the cowards stand aloof at bay:
Sell every man his life as dear as mine,
And they shall find dear deer of us, my friends.
God and Saint George, Talbot and England's right,

Prosper our colors in this dangerous fight!

*[Exeunt.]*

*and my drums shall play the music for your dreadful death.*

*He isn't lying; I can hear the enemy:*
*some of you light cavalry, go out and investigate their forces.*
*Oh, what stupid carelessness!*
*Here we are, a little herd of England's*
*frightened deer, surrounded by a fence,*
*terrified by a kennel full of French dogs!*
*If we are English deer, then let us show our ancestry;*
*we won't fall down at the first nip, like cowards,*
*we will be like the angry, mad and desperate stags,*
*that turn on the bloody hounds with our steel antlers*
*and make the cowards stand back barking:*
*if everyone sells his life as dearly as I shall sell mine,*
*they will find us to the expensive venison, my friends.*
*For God and Saint George, Talbot and the rights of England,*
*may our forces prosper in this dangerous fight!*

# SCENE III. Plains in Gascony.

*[Enter a Messenger that meets York. Enter York with trumpet and many soldiers.]*

YORK.
Are not the speedy scouts return'd again,
That dogg'd the mighty army of the Dauphin?

*Haven't the speedy scouts come back,
who were following the great army of the Dauphin?*

MESSENGER.
They are return'd, my lord, and give it out
That he is march'd to Bordeaux with his power,
To fight with Talbot: as he march'd along,
By your espials were discovered
Two mightier troops than that the Dauphin led,
Which join'd with him and made their march for
Bordeaux.

*They are back, my lord, and they tell us
that he has marched to Bordeaux with his forces,
to fight with Talbot: as he marched along,
your spies discovered
two larger forces than the one the Dauphin led,
which joined up with him and headed for
Bordeaux.*

YORK.
A plague upon that villain Somerset,
That thus delays my promised supply
Of horsemen, that were levied for this siege!
Renowned Talbot doth expect my aid,
And I am lowted by a traitor villain,
And cannot help the noble chevalier:
God comfort him in this necessity!
If he miscarry, farewell wars in France.

*Damn that villain Somerset
who hasn't provided me with the promised supply
of horsemen that were allocated for this siege!
Great Talbot is expecting my help,
and I am mocked by a traitorous villain,
and can't help the noble knight:
may God help him in his plight!
If he fails, that's the end of our French wars.*

*[Enter Sir William Lucy.]*

LUCY.
Thou princely leader of our English strength,
Never so needful on the earth of France,
Spur to the rescue of the noble Talbot,
Who now is girdled with a waist of iron,
And hemm'd about with grim destruction.
To Bordeaux, warlike Duke! to Bordeaux, York!
Else, farewell, Talbot, France, and England's honor.

*You princely leader of our English forces,
you were never more needed here in France,
ride to the rescue of the noble Talbot,
who is now encircled in an iron trap,
completely surrounded with grim destruction.
To Bordeaux, warlike duke! To Bordeaux, York!
Otherwise, that's the end of Talbot, France, and the
honour of England.*

YORK.
O God, that Somerset, who in proud heart
Doth stop my cornets, were in Talbot's place!
So should we save a valiant gentleman
By forfeiting a traitor and a coward.
Mad ire and wrathful fury makes me weep,
That thus we die, while remiss traitors sleep.

*Oh God, I wish that Somerset, who is arrogantly
keeping my forces from me, were in Talbot's place!
That way we could save a brave gentleman
by sacrificing a traitor and a coward.
Mad anger and fury makes me weep,
that we should die while neglectful traitors don't do their
duty.*

LUCY.
O, send some succor to the distress'd lord!

*Oh, send some help to the troubled Lord!*

YORK.
He dies; we lose; I break my warlike word;

*He shall die, we shall lose, I will break my military
promise;*

We mourn, France smiles; we lose, they daily get;

*we shall mourn, France shall smile; we shall lose, they
will gain by the day;*

All 'long of this vile traitor Somerset.

*all on account of this vile traitor Somerset.*

LUCY.
Then God take mercy on brave Talbot's soul;
And on his son young John, who two hours since
I met in travel toward his warlike father!
This seven years did not Talbot see his son;
And now they meet where both their lives are done.

*Then may God have mercy on the sole of brave Talbot;
and on that of his young son John, whom I met
two hours ago travelling towards his warlike father!
Talbot has not seen his son for the last seven years;
and now they will meet just as their lives end.*

YORK.
Alas, what joy shall noble Talbot have,
To bid his young son welcome to his grave?
Away! vexation almost stops my breath,
That sunder'd friends greet in the hour of death.
Lucy, farewell:  no more my fortune can,
But curse the cause I cannot aid the man.
Maine, Blois, Poictiers, and Tours, are won away,
'Long all of Somerset and his delay.

*Alas, is that the happiness noble Talbot has,
to welcome his young son to his grave?
Go! I almost can't breathe with sorrow,
that divided friends should meet at the hour of death.
Lucy, farewell: I can't help the man, all I can do
is curse the reason why.
Maine, Blois, Poitiers and Tours have all been lost,
thanks to Somerset and his delay.*

*[Exit, with his soldiers.]*

LUCY.
Thus, while the vulture of sedition
Feeds in the bosom of such great commanders,
Sleeping neglection doth betray to loss
The conquest of our scarce cold conqueror,

That ever living man of memory,
Henry the Fifth: whiles they each other cross,
Lives, honors, lands and all hurry to loss.

*So, while the vulture of rebellion
is eating at the heart of such great commanders,
lazy neglect has surrendered
the conquests of the conqueror who is hardly cold in his grave,
the man who lives forever in our memories,
Henry the Fifth: while they fight with each other,
lives, honour, lands and everything are lost.*

*[Exit.]*

# SCENE IV. Other plains in Gascony.

*[Enter Somerset, with his army; a Captain of Talbot's with him.]*

SOMERSET.
It is too late; I cannot send them now:
This expedition was by York and Talbot
Too rashly plotted: all our general force
Might with a sally of the very town
Be buckled with: the over-daring Talbot
Hath sullied all his gloss of former honor
By this unheedful, desperate, wild adventure:
York set him on to fight and die in shame,
That, Talbot dead, great York might bear the name.

*It's too late; I can't send them now:*
*York and Talbot launched this expedition*
*too hurriedly: all of our army*
*could be overcome just by an attack*
*of the townspeople: the reckless Talbot*
*has ruined the reputation which he previously gained*
*through this thoughtless, desperate and wild adventure:*
*York encouraged him to fight and die shamefully,*
*so that, with Talbot dead, great York might take his place.*

CAPTAIN.
Here is Sir William Lucy, who with me
Set from our o'er-match'd forces forth for aid.

*Here is Sir William Lucy, who came with me*
*from our outnumbered forces to find help.*

*[Enter Sir William Lucy.]*

SOMERSET.
How now, Sir William! whither were you sent?

*Hello there, Sir William! Where have you come from?*

LUCY.
Whither, my lord? from bought and sold Lord Talbot;
Who, ring'd about with bold adversity,
Cries out for noble York and Somerset,
To beat assailing death from his weak legions;
And whiles the honorable captain there
Drops bloody sweat from his war-wearied limbs,
And, in advantage lingering, looks for rescue,
You, his false hopes, the trust of England's honor,
Keep off aloof with worthless emulation.
Let not your private discord keep away
The levied succors that should lend him aid,
While he, renowned noble gentleman,
Yield up his life unto a world of odds.
Orleans the Bastard, Charles, Burgundy,
Alencon, Reignier, compass him about,
And Talbot perisheth by your default.

*Where, my lord? From the betrayed Lord Talbot;*
*who, surrounded by bold enemies,*
*is crying out for noble York and Somerset*
*to drive the deadly assault back from his weak forces;*
*and while the honourable captain is there*
*dripping bloody sweat from his exhausted limbs,*
*and, clinging to his last hope, looks for rescue,*
*you, his false hopes, the guardians of England's honour,*
*stay away and pursue your worthless struggles.*
*Don't let your private disagreement keep back*
*the forces that you should be sending to help him,*
*while he, that great noble gentleman,*
*gives up his life against overwhelming odds.*
*Orleans the bastard, Charles, Burgundy,*
*Alencon, Reignier, all surround him,*
*and Talbot will die and it will be your fault.*

SOMERSET.
York set him on; York should have sent him aid.

*York encouraged him; York should have sent him help.*

LUCY.
And York as fast upon your grace exclaims;
Swearing that you withhold his levied host,
Collected for this expedition.

*And York complains just as passionately about your grace;*
*he swears that you have held back his army,*
*which was raised for this expedition.*

SOMERSET.
York lies; he might have sent and had the horse:

I owe him little duty, and less love;
And take foul scorn to fawn on him by sending.

*York is lying; he could have asked for the cavalry and he*
*would have had them:*
*I don't owe him any duty, and less love;*
*I wasn't going to crawl to him by sending them unasked.*

LUCY.
The fraud of England, not the force of France,
Hath now entrapp'd the noble-minded Talbot:
Never to England shall he bear his life;
But dies, betray'd to fortune by your strife.

*It's the fraud of England, not the force of France,*
*that has trapped the noble minded Talbot:*
*he shall never come back to England alive;*
*he dies, abandoned to his fate by your arguments.*

SOMERSET.
Come, go; I will dispatch the horsemen straight:
Within six hours they will be at his aid.

*Come, let's go; I will send cavalry at once:*
*they shall be there to help him within six hours.*

LUCY.
Too late comes rescue; he is ta'en or slain;
For fly he could not, if he would have fled;
And fly would Talbot never, though he might.

*The rescue comes too late; he will be captured or killed;*
*for he couldn't escape, even if he wanted to;*
*and Talbot would never run, even if he had the chance.*

SOMERSET.
If he be dead, brave Talbot, then adieu!

*If he is dead, then farewell, brave Talbot!*

LUCY.
His fame lives in the world, his shame in you.

*His fame lives on in the world, the shame is all yours.*

*[Exeunt.]*

# SCENE V. The English camp near Bordeaux.

*[Enter Talbot and John his son.]*

TALBOT.
O young John Talbot! I did send for thee
To tutor thee in stratagems of war,
That Talbot's name might be in thee revived
When sapless age and weak unable limbs
Should bring thy father to his drooping chair.
But, O malignant and ill-boding stars!
Now thou art come unto a feast of death,
A terrible and unavoided danger:
Therefore, dear boy, mount on my swiftest horse;
And I'll direct thee how thou shalt escape
By sudden flight:  come, dally not, be gone.

JOHN.
Is my name Talbot? and am I your son?
And shall I fly? O, if you love my mother,
Dishonor not her honorable name,
To make a bastard and a slave of me!
The world will say, he is not Talbot's blood,
That basely fled when noble Talbot stood.

TALBOT.
Fly, to revenge my death, if I be slain.

JOHN.
He that flies so will ne'er return again.

TALBOT.
If we both stay, we both are sure to die.

JOHN.
Then let me stay; and, father, do you fly;
Your loss is great, so your regard should be;
My worth unknown, no loss is known in me.
Upon my death the French can little boast;
In yours they will, in you all hopes are lost.

Flight cannot stain the honor you have won;
But mine it will, that no exploit have done;
You fled for vantage, every one will swear;
But, if I bow, they 'll say it was for fear.
There is no hope that ever I will stay,
If the first hour I shrink and run away.
Here on my knee I beg mortality,
Rather than life preserved with infamy.

TALBOT.
Shall all thy mother's hopes lie in one tomb?

JOHN.
Aye, rather than I 'll shame my mother's womb.

*Oh young John Talbot! I sent for you*
*to teach you the business of war,*
*so that you could bear the name of Talbot*
*when weak old age and strengthless limbs*
*confined your father to his invalid chair.*
*But oh, what a terrible fate!*
*You have come to a feast of death,*
*a terrible and unavoidable danger:*
*so, dear boy, take my swiftest horse;*
*and I shall tell you how to escape*
*in a sudden flight. Come, don't waste time, go.*

*Is my name Talbot? And am I your son?*
*And shall I flee? Oh, if you love my mother,*
*do not dishonour her honourable name,*
*by making a bastard and a slave out of me!*
*The world will say, he cannot have been Talbot's son,*
*because he ran away when noble Talbot didn't.*

*Flee, and revenge my death, if I am killed.*

*Anyone who flees like that will never come back.*

*If we both stay, we are both certain to die.*

*Then let me stay, and you, father, flee;*
*you are so well regarded your loss would be huge,*
*nobody knows me, nobody would miss me.*
*The French couldn't boast about killing me;*
*they will boast about you, and all hopes will be lost if you*
*die.*
*Running away cannot tarnish the honour you have won;*
*but it will tarnish mine, who has done nothing;*
*everyone will swear that you fled out of strategy;*
*but, if I do it, they'll say it's because I was scared.*
*There's no hope that I would ever stand in a battle,*
*if I run away in my first hour of one.*
*I beg you on my knees to let me die,*
*rather than live badly thought of.*

*Shall everything your mother loves lie in one tomb?*

*Sooner that than that I should make her ashamed.*

TALBOT.
Upon my blessing, I command thee go.

*I give you my blessing and order you to go.*

JOHN.
To fight I will, but not to fly the foe.

*I will go to fight, but not to escape the enemy.*

TALBOT.
Part of thy father may be saved in thee.

*Part of your father might be preserved in you.*

JOHN.
No part of him but will be shame in me.

*Any part which survived would be ashamed of me.*

TALBOT.
Thou never hadst renown, nor canst not lose it.

*You never had any fame, so you can't lose it.*

JOHN.
Yes, your renowned name: shall flight abuse it?

*I have your famous name: shall I tarnish it by fleeing?*

TALBOT.
Thy father's charge shall clear thee from that stain.

*Your father's orders will absolve you from that accusation.*

JOHN.
You cannot witness for me, being slain.
If death be so apparent, then both fly.

*You will be dead and won't be able to bear witness for me.*
*If death is so obvious, let's both run.*

TALBOT.
And leave my followers here to fight and die;
My age was never tainted with such shame.

*That would leave my followers here to fight and die;*
*I would never allow such shame on my age.*

JOHN.
And shall my youth be guilty of such blame?
No more can I be sever'd from your side,
Than can yourself yourself in twain divide:
Stay, go, do what you will, the like do I;
For live I will not, if my father die.

*But I have to have it on my youth?*
*I can't be taken from your side,*
*any more than you could split yourself in two:*
*stay, go, do what you want, I shall do the same;*
*for I will not live, if my father dies.*

TALBOT.
Then here I take my leave of thee, fair son,
Born to eclipse thy life this afternoon.
Come, side by side together live and die;
And soul with soul from France to heaven fly.

*Then I shall part from you here, fair son,*
*born to lose your life this afternoon.*
*Come, we shall live and die together, side by side;*
*and our souls shall fly together from France to heaven.*

[Exeunt.]

# SCENE VI. A field of battle.

*[Alarum: excursions, wherein Talbot's Son is hemmed about, and Talbot rescues him.]*

TALBOT.
Saint George and victory; fight, soldiers, fight:
The regent hath with Talbot broke his word,
And left us to the rage of France his sword.
Where is John Talbot? Pause, and take thy breath;
I gave thee life and rescued thee from death.

JOHN.
O, twice my father, twice am I thy son!
The life thou gavest me first was lost and done,
Till with thy warlike sword, despite of fate,
To my determined time thou gavest new date.

TALBOT.
When from the Dauphin's crest thy sword struck fire,
It warm'd thy father's heart with proud desire
Of bold-faced victory. Then leaden age,
Quicken'd with youthful spleen and warlike rage,
Beat down Alencon, Orleans, Burgundy,
And from the pride of Gallia rescued thee.
The ireful bastard Orleans, that drew blood
From thee, my boy, and had the maidenhood
Of thy first fight, I soon encountered,
And interchanging blows I quickly shed
Some of his bastard blood; and in disgrace
Bespoke him thus; 'Contaminated base
And misbegotten blood I spill of thine,
Mean and right poor, for that pure blood of mine,
Which thou didst force from Talbot, my brave boy:'
Here, purposing the Bastard to destroy,
Came in strong rescue. Speak, thy father's care,
Art thou not weary, John? how dost thou fare?
Wilt thou yet leave the battle, boy, and fly,
Now thou art seal'd the son of chivalry?
Fly, to revenge my death when I am dead:
The help of one stands me in little stead.
O, too much folly is it, well I wot,
To hazard all our lives in one small boat!
If I to-day die not with Frenchmen's rage,
To-morrow I shall die with mickle age:
By me they nothing gain an if I stay;
'Tis but the short'ning of my life one day:
In thee thy mother dies, our household's name,
My death's revenge, thy youth, and England's fame:

All these and more we hazard by thy stay;
All these are saved if thou wilt fly away.

JOHN.
The sword of Orleans hath not made me smart;
These words of yours draw life-blood from my heart:

---

*Fight, soldiers, fight for St George and victory;*
*the Regent has broken his promise to Talbot,*
*and left us to face the anger of France.*
*Where is John Talbot? Pause, and catch your breath.*
*I gave you life, and I rescued you from death.*

*Oh, you are twice my father, I am twice your son!*
*I had lost the first life you gave me,*
*until your warlike sword, rebelling against fate,*
*set a new date for the time of my death.*

*When your sword struck sparks from the Dauphin's helmet*
*it warmed your father's heart with proud desire*
*of startling victories then slow age,*
*enlivened by youthful anger and warlike rage*
*smashed down Alencon, Orleans, Burgundy,*
*and rescued you from the pride of France.*
*That angry bastard of Orleans, who drew blood*
*from you, my boy, and was the one who faced you*
*in your very first fight, I soon came across,*
*and, exchanging blows, I quickly shed*
*some of his bastard blood, and to insult him*
*I spoke these words to him: "I am going to spill*
*your contaminated lowly bastard blood,*
*mean and poor, in exchange for the pure blood of mine*
*which you spilt of my brave lad Talbot's."*
*Then, as I meant to destroy the bastard,*
*a strong force came to rescue him. Tell me, as your father:*
*are you not tired, John? How are you?*
*Why not now leave the battle, boy, and flee,*
*now you have proved your chivalry?*
*Flee, to revenge my death when I am dead;*
*the help of just one will not be much help to me.*
*I know perfectly well that it would be stupid*
*to risk all our lives in just one boat.*
*If I do not die today at the hand of an angry Frenchman,*
*tomorrow I shall die of old age.*
*They will gain nothing by killing me, and if I stay,*
*I will only be shortening my life by a day;*
*if you die so will your mother, the name of our family,*
*revenge for my death, your youth and the honour of*
*England.*
*We are risking all these and more by you staying;*
*all these will be saved, if you flee.*

*The sword of Orleans didn't hurt me;*
*these words of yours suck the lifeblood from my heart:*

On that advantage, bought with such a shame,
To save a paltry life and slay bright fame,
Before young Talbot from old Talbot fly,
The coward horse that bears me fall and die!
And like me to the peasant boys of France,
To be shame's scorn and subject of mischance!
Surely, by all the glory you have won,
An if I fly, I am not Talbot's son;
Then talk no more of flight, it is no boot;
If son to Talbot, die at Talbot's foot.

TALBOT.
Then follow thou thy desperate sire of Crete,
Thou Icarus; thy life to me is sweet:
If thou wilt fight, fight by thy father's side;
And, commendable proved, let 's die in pride.

*[Exeunt.]*

*shall I save my own life at the price*
*of your death and reputation?*
*Before young Talbot runs from old Talbot,*
*may the coward horse that carries me fall and die!*
*Compare me to the peasant boys of France,*
*mock me with shame, and may fate punish me.*
*Surely, through all the glory you have won,*
*if I fly then I am not your son.*
*So talk no more of flight, it's no use:*
*if I am the son of Talbot, I shall die with Talbot.*

*Then follow your desperate father of Crete,*
*you Icarus; your life is dear to me:*
*if you want to fight, fight by your father's side;*
*and, having proved our bravery, we shall die proud men.*

# SCENE VII. Another part of the field.

*[Alarum: excursions. Enter old Talbot led by a Servant.]*

TALBOT.
Where is my other life? mine own is gone;
O, where's young Talbot? where is valiant John?
Triumphant death, smear'd with captivity,
Young Talbot's valor makes me smile at thee:
When he perceived me shrink and on my knee,
His bloody sword he brandish'd over me,
And, like a hungry lion, did commence
Rough deeds of rage and stern impatience;
But when my angry guardant stood alone,
Tendering my ruin and assail'd of none,
Dizzy-ey'd fury and great rage of heart
Suddenly made him from my side to start
Into the clustering battle of the French;
And in that sea of blood my boy did drench
His over-mounting spirit, and there died,
My Icarus, my blossom, in his pride.

*Where is my other life? I have lost mine;*
*oh where is young Talbot? Where is brave John?*
*Triumphant death, who has me in your grasp,*
*young Talbot's bravery makes me smile at you:*
*when he saw me drop down onto my knees,*
*he waved his bloody sword over me,*
*and, like a hungry lion, began*
*great deeds of rage and stern defiance.*
*But when my angry protector stood alone,*
*taking care of my downfall and attacked by none,*
*wild eyed anger and a great rage in his heart*
*made him suddenly run from my side*
*into the gathering group of French soldiers,*
*and in that sea of blood my boy drowned*
*his overwhelming spirit, and there he died,*
*my Icarus, my offspring, in his pride.*

SERVANT.
O my dear lord, lo where your son is borne!

*O my dear lord, look, they are carrying your son!*

*[Enter soldiers, with the body of young Talbot.]*

TALBOT.
Thou antic Death, which laugh'st us here to scorn,
Anon, from thy insulting tyranny,
Coupled in bonds of perpetuity,
Two Talbots, winged through the lither sky,
In thy despite shall 'scape mortality.
O thou, whose wounds become hard-favor'd death,
Speak to thy father ere thou yield thy breath!
Brave death by speaking, whether he will or no;

Imagine him a Frenchman and thy foe.
Poor boy! he smiles, methinks, as who should say,
Had death been French, then death had died to-day.

Come, come and lay him in his father's arms:
My spirit can no longer bear these harms.
Soldiers, adieu! I have what I would have,
Now my old arms are young John Talbot's grave.

*You jester death, who mocks us with his laughter,*
*soon, two Talbots shall fly through the yielding sky,*
*joined together forever,*
*flying away from your insulting tyranny,*
*escaping mortality in spite of you.*
*Oh you, whose wounds are certainly mortal,*
*speak to your father before you stop breathing!*
*Out face death by speaking, whether he wants you to or*
*not;*
*imagine he's a Frenchman, and your enemy.*
*Poor boy! He smiles, I think, as if he's saying,*
*if death had been French, then death would have died*
*today.*
*Come, come and put him in his father's arms:*
*my spirit can no longer tolerate this misery.*
*Soldiers, farewell! I have everything I want,*
*now that my old arms make a grave for young John*
*Talbot.*

*[Dies.]*

*[Enter Charles, Alencon, Burgundy, Bastard, La Pucelle, and forces.]*

CHARLES.
Had York and Somerset brought rescue in,
We should have found a bloody day of this.

*If York and Somerset had come to the rescue,*
*we should have had a bloody time of it.*

BASTARD.

How the young whelp of Talbot's, raging-wood,
Did flesh his puny sword in Frenchmen's blood!

PUCELLE.
Once I encounter'd him, and thus I said:
'Thou maiden youth, be vanquish'd by a maid.'
But, with a proud majestical high scorn,
He answer'd thus: 'Young Talbot was not born
To be the pillage of a giglot wench:'
So, rushing in the bowels of the French,
He left me proudly, as unworthy fight.

BURGUNDY.
Doubtless he would have made a noble knight:
See, where he lies inhearsed in the arms
Of the most bloody nurser of his harms!

BASTARD.
Hew them to pieces, hack their bones asunder,
Whose life was England's glory, Gallia's wonder.

CHARLES.
O, no, forbear! for that which we have fled
During the life, let us not wrong it dead.

*[Enter Sir William Lucy, attended; Herald of the French preceding.]*

LUCY.
Herald, conduct me to the Dauphin's tent,
To know who hath obtain'd the glory of the day.

CHARLES.
On what submissive message art thou sent?

LUCY.
Submission, Dauphin! 'tis a mere French word;
We English warriors wot not what it means.
I come to know what prisoners thou hast ta'en,
And to survey the bodies of the dead.

CHARLES.
For prisoners ask'st thou? hell our prison is.

But tell me whom thou seek'st.

LUCY.
But where's the great Alcides of the field,

Valiant Lord Talbot, Earl of Shrewsbury,
Created for his rare success in arms,
Great Earl of Washford, Waterford, and Valence;
Lord Talbot of Goodrig and Urchinfield,
Lord Strange of Blackmere, Lord Verdun of Alton,
Lord Cromwell of Wingfield, Lord Furnival of Sheffield,
The thrice-victorious Lord of Falconbridge;

---

*How that young puppy of Talbot's, raging mad,
covered his little sword with the blood of Frenchmen.*

*I came across him once, and I said to him,
"You virgin youth, be beaten by a virgin."
But, with a proud majestic haughty arrogance,
he answered me thus: "Young Talbot wasn't born
to be the victim of a lower class slut."
So, rushing into the heart of the French forces,
he left me proudly, as an unworthy opponent.*

*No doubt he would have made a noble knight:
look, where he is lying dead in the arms
of the one who caused all this bloodshed!*

*Hack them to pieces, tear their bones apart,
their life was the glory of England, the amazement of France.*

*Oh no, hold off! Let's not insult when dead
what we fled in life.*

*Herald, take me to the tent of the Dauphin,
to find out what has happened today.*

*What humble message have you been sent with?*

*Humble, Dauphin! That's just a French word;
we English warriors don't know what it means.
I have come to ask what prisoners you have captured,
and to count the bodies of the dead.*

*You're asking for prisoners? We send our prisoners to hell.
But tell me who you are looking for.*

*I want to know where the great Hercules of the battlefield is,
Brave Lord Talbot, Earl of Shrewsbury,
ennobled for his great success in battle,
Great Earl of Washford, Waterford, and Valence;
Lord Talbot of Goodrig and Urchinfield,
Lord Strange of Blackmere, Lord Verdun of Alton,
Lord Cromwell of Wingfield, Lord Furnival of Sheffield,
The thrice-victorious Lord of Falconbridge;*

Knight of the noble order of Saint George,
Worthy Saint Michael, and the Golden Fleece;
Great marshal to Henry the Sixth
Of all his wars within the realm of France?

PUCELLE.
Here's a silly stately style indeed!
The Turk, that two and fifty kingdoms hath,
Writes not so tedious a style as this.
Him that thou magnifiest with all these titles
Stinking and fly-blown lies here at our feet.

LUCY.
Is Talbot slain, the Frenchman's only scourge,
Your kingdom's terror and black Nemesis?
O, were mine eye-balls into bullets turn'd,
That I in rage might shoot them at your faces!
O, that I could but call these dead to life!
It were enough to fright the realm of France:
Were but his picture left amongst you here,
It would amaze the proudest of you all.
Give me their bodies, that I may bear them hence
And give them burial as beseems their worth.

PUCELLE.
I think this upstart is old Talbot's ghost,
He speaks with such a proud commanding spirit,
For God's sake, let him have 'em; to keep them here,
They would but stink, and putrify the air.

CHARLES.
Go, take their bodies hence.

LUCY.
I 'll bear them hence; but from their ashes shall be rear'd
A phoenix that shall make all France afeard.

CHARLES.
So we be rid of them, do with 'em what thou wilt.

And now to Paris, in this conquering vein:
All will be ours, now bloody Talbot's slain.

*[Exeunt.]*

Knight of the noble order of Saint George,
Worthy Saint Michael, and the Golden Fleece;
Great marshal to Henry the Sixth
in all his wars within the great realm of France?

Here's a stupid stately way of talking!
The Turk, who has fifty two kingdoms,
doesn't write in such a tedious style as this.
The person that you enlarge with all those titles
is lying here stinking and covered in flies at our feet.

Has Talbot been killed, the great punisher of the French,
the terror of your kingdom and your black nemesis?
Oh, I wish my eyeballs would turn into bullets,
so in my anger I could shoot them in your faces!
Oh, if I could only call these dead back to life!
It would be enough to terrify the country of France
if we just left his picture amongst you,
it would confuse the most arrogant of you.
Give me their bodies, so I can take them away
and give them the burial they deserve.

I think this upstart is the ghost of old Talbot,
he has such a bossy arrogant way of speaking.
For God's sake, let him take them; if we keep them here
they will just stink and spread infection.

Go, take their bodies away.

I'll take them away; but a Phoenix shall rise from their ashes
that will terrify all of France.

As long as we are rid of them, do what you want with them.
And now we shall go to Paris, to continue our conquest:
we shall have everything, now that bloody Talbot is dead.

# Act V

## SCENE I. London. The palace.

*[Sennet. Enter King, Gloucester, and Exeter.]*

KING.
Have you perused the letters from the pope,
The emperor, and the Earl of Armagnac?

*Have you read letters from the Pope,*
*the Emperor and the Earl of Armagnac?*

GLOUCESTER.
I have, my lord:  and their intent is this:
They humbly sue unto your excellence
To have a godly peace concluded of
Between the realms of England and of France.

*I have, my lord: and this is what they say:*
*they humbly entreat your Majesty*
*to arrange a godly peace*
*between the kingdoms of England and France.*

KING.
How doth your grace affect their motion?

*And what does your grace think of their request?*

GLOUCESTER.
Well, my good lord; and as the only means
To stop effusion of our Christian blood
And stablish quietness on every side.

*I like it, my good lord, as the only way*
*to stop more Christian blood being spilled*
*and to settle calm on each side.*

KING.
Aye, marry, uncle; for I always thought
It was both impious and unnatural
That such immanity and bloody strife
Should reign among professors of one faith.

*Yes indeed, uncle; I have always thought*
*it was both unnatural and impious*
*that such enmity and bloody strife*
*should rule amongst people from the same faith.*

GLOUCESTER.
Beside, my lord, the sooner to effect
And surer bind this knot of amity,
The Earl of Armagnac, near knit to Charles,
A man of great authority in France,
Proffers his only daughter to your grace
In marriage, with a large and sumptuous dowry.

*Besides, my lord, in order to speed up*
*and make firmer this bond of friendship,*
*the Earl of Armagnac, closely related to Charles,*
*a man of very high position in France,*
*offers his only daughter to your Grace*
*in marriage, with a large and rich dowry.*

KING.
Marriage, uncle! alas, my years are young!
And fitter is my study and my books
Than wanton dalliance with a paramour.
Yet call the ambassadors; and, as you please,
So let them have their answers every one:
I shall be well content with any choice
Tends to God's glory and my country's weal.

*Marriage, uncle! Alas, I am still young!*
*I'm more suited to schoolwork and my books*
*than to loose carrying on with a lover.*
*But call in the ambassadors and give them*
*the answers you think appropriate:*
*I will be happy with any choice*
*that enhances the glory of God and my country's fortunes.*

*[Enter Winchester in Cardinal's habit, a Legate and two Ambassadors.]*

EXETER.
What! is my Lord of Winchester install'd
And call'd unto a cardinal's degree?
Then I perceive that will be verified

*What! Has my Lord of Winchester been*
*appointed as a cardinal?*
*Then I see that what Henry the Fifth*

Henry the Fifth did sometime prophesy,
'If once he come to be a cardinal,
He'll make his cap co-equal with the crown.'

*once prophesied will come true:*
*"If he ever becomes a cardinal,*
*he'll make his position equal with the Crown."*

KING.
My lords ambassadors, your several suits
Have been consider'd and debated on.
Your purpose is both good and reasonable;
And therefore are we certainly resolved
To draw conditions of a friendly peace;
Which by my Lord of Winchester we mean
Shall be transported presently to France.

*My lords ambassadors, your different requests*
*have been considered and debated.*
*What you ask is both good and reasonable;*
*so we have certainly decided*
*that we will draw up a peace treaty;*
*I intend my Lord of Winchester*
*to take it to France at once.*

GLOUCESTER.
And for the proffer of my lord your master,
I have inform'd his highness so at large,
As liking of the lady's virtuous gifts,
Her beauty and the value of her dower,
He doth intend she shall be England's Queen.

*As for the offer to my Lord from your master,*
*I have informed his Highness of it,*
*and admiring the lady's goodness and accomplishments,*
*her beauty and the value of her dowry,*
*he has decided that she shall be England's Queen.*

KING.
In argument and proof of which contract,
Bear her this jewel, pledge of my affection.
And so, my lord protector, see them guarded
And safely brought to Dover; where inshipp'd,
Commit them to the fortune of the sea.

*And to seal and give proof of this decision,*
*take this jewel as a token of my affection.*
*And so, my lord protector, make sure they are escorted*
*safely to Dover, get them on their ship*
*and give them to the fortune of the sea.*

*[Exeunt all but Winchester and Legate.]*

WINCHESTER.
Stay my lord legate:  you shall first receive
The sum of money which I promised
Should be deliver'd to his holiness
For clothing me in these grave ornaments.

*Wait my lord legate: you must have*
*the sum of money which I promised*
*would be given to the Pope*
*for appointing me cardinal.*

LEGATE.
I will attend upon your lordship's leisure.

*I shall be ready whenever your lordship is.*

WINCHESTER.
*[Aside]* Now Winchester will not submit, I trow,
Or be inferior to the proudest peer.
Humphrey of Gloucester, thou shalt well perceive
That neither in birth or for authority,
The bishop will be overborne by thee:
I 'll either make thee stoop and bend thy knee,
Or sack this country with a mutiny.

*Now I don't believe that Winchester will agree*
*to be inferior to any of the peers.*
*Humphrey of Gloucester, you shall see*
*that the bishop will not be below you,*
*in position or power:*
*I'll either make you bow down to me,*
*or start a civil war in this country.*

*[Exeunt.]*

# SCENE II. France. Plains in Anjou.

*[Enter Charles, Burgundy, Alencon, Bastard, Reignier, La Pucelle, and forces.]*

CHARLES.
These news, my lords, may cheer our drooping spirits:
'Tis said the stout Parisians do revolt
And turn again unto the warlike French.

*This news, my lords, may raise our drooping spirits:
it's said that the strong Parisians are rebelling
and becoming warlike Frenchmen again.*

ALENCON.
Then march to Paris, royal Charles of France,
And keep not back your powers in dalliance.

*Then march to Paris, royal Charles of France,
and don't hold back your forces here.*

PUCELLE.
Peace be amongst them, if they turn to us;
Else, ruin combat with their palaces!

*May peace be with them, if they join with us;
otherwise, may all their palaces fall in war!*

*[Enter Scout.]*

SCOUT.
Success unto our valiant general,
And happiness to his accomplices!

*May our brave general have success,
and may his accomplices be happy!*

CHARLES.
What tidings send our scouts? I prithee, speak.

*What news do our scouts send? Please, speak.*

SCOUT.
The English army, that divided was
Into two parties, is now conjoin'd in one,
And means to give you battle presently.

*The English army, that was split
into two parties, has now joined into one,
and means to do battle with you at once.*

CHARLES.
Somewhat too sudden, sirs, the warning is;
But we will presently provide for them.

*This is a little too early for us, sirs;
but we will get ourselves ready for them.*

BURGUNDY.
I trust the ghost of Talbot is not there:
Now he is gone, my lord, you need not fear.

*I hope the ghost of Talbot isn't there;
now he has gone, my lord, you have nothing to fear.*

PUCELLE.
Of all base passions, fear is most accursed.
Command the conquest, Charles, it shall be thine,
Let Henry fret and all the world repine.

*Of all the low emotions, fear is the worst.
Order the victory, Charles, it shall be yours,
let Henry worry and all the world grieve.*

CHARLES.
Then on, my lords; and France be fortunate!

*Then forward, my lords; may fortune favour France!*

*[Exeunt.]*

## SCENE III. Before Angiers.

*[Alarum. Excursions. Enter La Pucelle.]*

PUCELLE.
The regent conquers, and the Frenchmen fly.
Now help, ye charming spells and periapts;
And ye choice spirits that admonish me,
And give me signs of future accidents. *[Thunder]*
You speedy helpers, that are substitutes
Under the lordly monarch of the north,
Appear and aid me in this enterprise.

*[Enter Fiends.]*

This speedy and quick appearance argues proof
Of your accustom'd diligence to me.
Now, ye familiar spirits, that are cull'd
Out of the powerful regions under earth,
Help me this once, that France may get the field.

*[They walk and speak not.]*

O, hold me not with silence over-long!
Where I was wont to feed you with my blood,
I 'll lop a member off and give it you
In earnest of a further benefit,
So you do condescend to help me now.

*[They hang their heads.]*

No hope to have redress? My body shall
Pay recompense, if you will grant my suit.

*[They shake their heads.]*

Cannot my body nor blood-sacrifice
Entreat you to your wonted furtherance?
Then take my soul, my body, soul and all,
Before that England give the French the foil.

*[They depart.]*

See, they forsake me!  Now the time is come
That France must vail her lofty-plumed crest,
And let her head fall into England's lap.
My ancient incantations are too weak,
And hell too strong for me to buckle with:
Now, France, thy glory droopeth to the dust.

*[Exit.]*

*[Excursions. Re-enter La Pucelle fighting hand to hand with York: La Pucelle is taken. The French fly.]*

---

*The Regent has won and the Frenchmen are fleeing.*
*Now help, you enchanting spells and charms,*
*and you, great spirits who warn me*
*and give me indications of future events.*
*You speedy helpers, who are substitutes*
*for your lord the devil,*
*appear, and help me in this enterprise.*

*Enter fiends.*

*The speed with which you appeared proves*
*that you are used to working for me.*
*Now, you familiar spirits, which come*
*from the powerful regions under the earth,*
*help me this one time, so that France can win the battle.*

*They walk, and do not speak.*

*Do not keep me in silence for too long:*
*where I used to offer you my blood,*
*I'll chop a limb off and give it to you*
*as a token of further payment*
*if you help me now.*

*They hang their heads.*

*Is there no hope of help? You can have my*
*body in payment if you grant my request.*

*They shake their heads.*

*Can't my body or a blood sacrifice*
*persuade you to give your usual assistance?*
*Then take my soul—my body, soul, all of me—*
*before the French triumph over the English.*

*They leave.*

*See, they are leaving me. Now the time has come*
*that France must lower her high plumed crest,*
*and let her head fall into England's lap.*
*My ancient spells are too weak,*
*and hell is too strong for me to force to my will.*
*Now, France, your glory has fallen to the dust.*

YORK.
Damsel of France, I think I have you fast:
Unchain your spirits now with spelling charms,
And try if they can gain your liberty.
A goodly prize, fit for the devil's grace!
See, how the ugly witch doth bend her brows,
As if with Circe she would change my shape!

*Lady of France, I think I have you in my power:*
*unleash your spirits now with your spells,*
*and see if they can gain your freedom.*
*A good prize, suitable for the Devil's favour!*
*See how the ugly witch frowns,*
*as if she would like to change my shape, as Circe did!*

PUCELLE.
Chang'd to a worser shape thou canst not be.

*You can't be changed to a worse shape.*

YORK.
O, Charles the Dauphin is a proper man;
No shape but his can please your dainty eye.

*Oh, Charles the Dauphin is a good man;*
*only his shape can please your choosy eye!*

PUCELLE.
A plaguing mischief light on Charles and thee!
And may ye both be suddenly surprised
By bloody hands, in sleeping on your beds!

*May a horrible plague fall on Charles and you!*
*And may you both be suddenly surprised*
*by bloody hands, when you're asleep!*

YORK.
Fell banning hag; enchantress, hold thy tongue!

*You foul cursing hag; you witch, hold your tongue!*

PUCELLE.
I prithee, give me leave to curse awhile.

*Please, allow me to curse for a while.*

YORK.
Curse, miscreant, when thou comest to the stake.

*You can curse, you criminal, when you are burnt at the stake.*

[Exeunt.]

[Alarum. Enter Suffolk, with Margaret in his hand.]

SUFFOLK.
Be what thou wilt, thou art my prisoner.

*Whoever you are, you are my prisoner.*

[Gazes on her.]

O fairest beauty, do not fear nor fly!
For I will touch thee but with reverent hands;
I kiss these fingers for eternal peace,
And lay them gently on thy tender side.
Who art thou? say, that I may honor thee.

*Oh you great beauty, do not be afraid or try and run!*
*I will only touch you with worshipping hands;*
*I kiss your fingers wishing you eternal peace,*
*and lay them gently by your sweet side.*
*Who are you? Say, so I can worship you.*

MARGARET.
Margaret my name, and daughter to a king,
The King of Naples, whosoe'er thou art.

*Margaret is my name, and I am the daughter of the King,*
*the King of Naples, whoever you are.*

SUFFOLK.
An earl I am, and Suffolk am I call'd.
Be not offended, nature's miracle,
Thou art allotted to be ta'en by me.
So doth the swan her downy cygnets save,
Keeping them prisoner underneath her wings.
Yet, if this servile usage once offend,
Go and be free again as Suffolk's friend.

*I am an earl, I am called Suffolk.*
*Don't be offended, miracle of nature;*
*I have been ordered to escort you.*
*This is how the swan protects its downy cygnets,*
*keeping them sheltered under its wings.*
*But, if my worshipful behaviour offends you,*
*go, and you can live freely as my friend.*

*[She is going.]*

O, stay! I have no power to let her pass;
My hand would free her, but my heart says no.
As plays the sun upon the glassy streams,
Twinkling another counterfeited beam,
So seems this gorgeous beauty to mine eyes.
Fain would I woo her, yet I dare not speak:
I'll call for pen and ink, and write my mind.
Fie, de la Pole! disable not thyself;
Hast not a tongue? is she not here?
Wilt thou be daunted at a woman's sight?
Aye, beauty's princely majesty is such,
Confounds the tongue and makes the senses rough.

MARGARET.
Say, Earl of Suffolk,--if thy name be so--
What ransom must I pay before I pass?
For I perceive I am thy prisoner.

SUFFOLK.
How canst thou tell she will deny thy suit,
Before thou make a trial of her love?

MARGARET.
Why speak'st thou not? what ransom must I pay?

SUFFOLK.
She's beautiful and therefore to be woo'd;
She is a woman, therefore to be won.

MARGARET.
Wilt thou accept of ransom? yea, or no.

SUFFOLK.
Fond man, remember that thou hast a wife;
Then how can Margaret be thy paramour?

MARGARET.
I were best leave him, for he will not hear.

SUFFOLK.
There all is marr'd; there lies a cooling card.

MARGARET.
He talks at random; sure, the man is mad.

SUFFOLK.
And yet a dispensation may be had.

MARGARET.
And yet I would that you would answer me.

SUFFOLK.
I'll win this Lady Margaret. For whom?
Why, for my king; tush, that 's a wooden thing!

---

*Oh stay! I have no power to set her free.*
*My hand wants to free her, but my heart says no.*
*This gorgeous beauty seems to me to look*
*like the sun playing on a glassy stream,*
*twinkling with its reflection.*
*I should like to woo her, but I dare not speak.*
*I'll order pen and ink and write down what I'm thinking.*
*Come, de la Pole, don't put yourself down:*
*haven't you got a tongue? Isn't she here?*
*Will you be daunted by the sight of a woman?*
*Yes. The royal majesty of beauty is so great*
*that it defeats the tongue, and confuses the senses.*

*Tell me, Earl of Suffolk--if that's your name--*
*what ransom must I pay before I can go?*
*For I see that I am your prisoner.*

*How do know that she will refuse you,*
*before you offer her your love?*

*Why won't you speak? What ransom must I pay?*

*She's beautiful, and therefore should be wooed;*
*she is a woman, and therefore she can be won.*

*Will you accept to ransom? Yes or no.*

*Stupid man, remember that you have a wife;*
*so how can Margaret be your lover?*

*I had better leave him, for he won't listen.*

*That spoils everything; that cools it all down.*

*He's talking randomly; I'm sure the man is mad.*

*And yet marriages can be dissolved.*

*And yet I should like you to answer me.*

*I'll win over this lady Margaret. Who for?*
*Why, for my king; pah, he's a wooden block!*

MARGARET.
He talks of wood:  it is some carpenter.

*He's talking of wood: he must be a carpenter.*

SUFFOLK.
Yet so my fancy may be satisfied,
And peace established between these realms.
But there remains a scruple in that too;
For though her father be the King of Naples,
Duke of Anjou and Maine, yet is he poor,
And our nobility will scorn the match.

*But in this way my desires could be fulfilled,*
*and peace could be established between these countries.*
*But there is a problem there too;*
*for although her father is the King of Naples,*
*Duke of Anjou and Maine, he is poor,*
*and our noblemen will reject the match.*

MARGARET.
Hear ye, captain, are you not at leisure?

*Can you hear me, captain, are you busy?*

SUFFOLK.
It shall be so, disdain they ne'er so much:
Henry is youthful and will quickly yield.
Madam, I have a secret to reveal.

*I shall do this, whatever they think:*
*Henry is young and will quickly submit.*
*Madam, I have a secret to tell you.*

MARGARET.
What though I be enthrall'd? he seems a knight,
And will not any way dishonor me.

*What if he wants to enslave me? He seems to be a knight,*
*and he won't do anything dishonourable.*

SUFFOLK.
Lady, vouchsafe to listen what I say.

*Lady, please listen to what I have to say.*

MARGARET.
Perhaps I shall be rescued by the French;
And then I need not crave his courtesy.

*Perhaps I will be rescued by the French;*
*and then I will not need to beg for his kindness.*

SUFFOLK.
Sweet madam, give me hearing in a cause--

*Sweet madam, listen to me about something–*

MARGARET.
Tush! women have been captivate ere now.

*Come! Women have been prisoners before now.*

SUFFOLK.
Lady, wherefore talk you so?

*Lady, why are you talking like this?*

MARGARET.
I cry you mercy, 'tis but Quid for Quo.

*I'm begging you for mercy, it's a fair exchange.*

SUFFOLK.
Say, gentle princess, would you not suppose
Your bondage happy, to be made a queen?

*Say, gentle Princess, if your imprisonment would*
*make you miserable, if you were a queen?*

MARGARET.
To be a queen in bondage is more vile
Than is a slave in base servility;
For princes should be free.

*To be a queen as a prisoner is more horrible*
*than to be a slave in service;*
*Princes should be free.*

SUFFOLK.
And so shall you,
If happy England's royal king be free.

*And so will you be,*
*if the royal king of happy England is.*

MARGARET.

Why, what concerns his freedom unto me? | *Why, what has his freedom got to do with me?*

SUFFOLK.
I'll undertake to make thee Henry's queen, | *I promise to make you Henry's Queen,*
To put a golden scepter in thy hand | *to put a golden sceptre in your hand*
And set a precious crown upon thy head, | *and a precious crown upon your head,*
If thou wilt condescend to be my-- | *if you agree to be my–*

MARGARET.
What? | *What?*

SUFFOLK.
His love. | *His love.*

MARGARET.
I am unworthy to be Henry's wife. | *I am not worthy of being Henry's wife.*

SUFFOLK.
No, gentle madam; I unworthy am | *No, sweet madam; I am unworthy*
To woo so fair a dame to be his wife, | *of wooing such a beautiful lady to be his wife,*
And have no portion in the choice myself. | *and I have no part in the choice myself.*
How say you, madam, are ye so content? | *What do you say, madam, would that make you happy?*

MARGARET.
An if my father please, I am content. | *If it pleases my father, I am happy.*

SUFFOLK.
Then call our captain and our colors forth. | *Then call our captain and put our banners out.*
And, madam, at your father's castle walls | *And, madam, we shall ask for a meeting*
We'll crave a parley, to confer with him. | *with your father at his castle walls.*

*[A parley sounded. Enter Reignier on the walls.]*

See, Reignier, see, thy daughter prisoner! | *Reignier, see your daughter is a prisoner!*

REIGNIER. To whom? | *Of whom?*

SUFFOLK.
To me. | *Of me.*

REIGNIER.
Suffolk, what remedy? | *Suffolk, what you want me to do?*
I am a soldier, and unapt to weep, | *I am a soldier, and I do not weep,*
Or to exclaim on fortune's fickleness. | *or curse my bad luck.*

SUFFOLK.
Yes, there is remedy enough, my lord: | *There is something you can do, my lord:*
Consent, and for thy honor give consent, | *you must give consent*
Thy daughter shall be wedded to my king; | *for your daughter to be married to my king;*
Whom I with pain have woo'd and won thereto; | *I have with difficulty wooed her and persuaded her to do that;*

And this her easy-held imprisonment | *and she can go from her comfortable imprisonment*
Hath gain'd thy daughter princely liberty. | *to a princely freedom.*

REIGNIER.
Speaks Suffolk as he thinks? | *Is Suffolk saying what he means?*

**SUFFOLK.**
Fair Margaret knows
That Suffolk doth not flatter, face, or feign.

*Fair Margaret knows*
*that Suffolk does not flatter or fake.*

**REIGNIER.**
Upon thy princely warrant, I descend
To give thee answer of thy just demand.

*With your princely guarantees, I shall come down*
*to answer your fair demand.*

*[Exit from the walls.]*

**SUFFOLK.**
And here I will expect thy coming.

*I shall wait for you here.*

*[Trumpets sound. Enter Reignier, below.]*

**REIGNIER.**
Welcome, brave earl, into our territories:
Command in Anjou what your honor pleases.

*Welcome, brave earl, to our lands:*
*in Anjou you can ask for whatever you please.*

**SUFFOLK.**
Thanks, Reignier, happy for so sweet a child,
Fit to be made companion with a king:
What answer makes your grace unto my suit?

*Thank you, Reignier, lucky to have such a sweet child,*
*who is fit to be a companion of King:*
*what answer does your grace make to my request?*

**REIGNIER.**
Since thou dost deign to woo her little worth
To be the princely bride of such a lord;
Upon condition I may quietly
Enjoy mine own, the country Maine and Anjou,
Free from oppression or the stroke of war,
My daughter shall be Henry's, if he please.

*Since you condescend to woo her in her lowly state*
*to be the bride of the King;*
*on condition that I may quietly*
*enjoy my own country of Maine and Anjou,*
*free from oppression or war,*
*my daughter shall marry Henry, if he wishes.*

**SUFFOLK.**
That is her ransom; I deliver her;
And those two counties I will undertake
Your Grace shall well and quietly enjoy.

*That is the ransom for her; I shall take her;*
*and I promise that these two regions*
*will be left alone for your Grace to quietly enjoy.*

**REIGNIER.**
And I again, in Henry's royal name,
As deputy unto that gracious king,
Give thee her hand, for sign of plighted faith.

*And in return I, in Henry's royal name,*
*as you are deputy to that gracious king,*
*give you her hand, to seal the engagement.*

**SUFFOLK.**
Reignier of France, I give thee kingly thanks,
Because this is in traffic of a king.
[Aside] And yet, methinks, I could be well content
To be mine own attorney in this case.
I'll over then to England with this news,
And make this marriage to be solemnized.
So, farewell, Reignier; set this diamond safe
In golden palaces, as it becomes.

*Reignier of France, I give you the thanks of the King,*
*because this is the King's business.*
*However, I think, I could be very happy*
*to work for myself in this case.*
*So I'll take this news over to England,*
*and have this marriage confirmed.*
*So, farewell, Reignier; keep this diamond safe*
*in the golden palaces it deserves.*

**REIGNIER.**
I do embrace thee as I would embrace
The Christian prince, King Henry, were he here.

*I embrace you as I would embrace*
*the Christian Prince, King Henry, if he were here.*

MARGARET.
Farewell, my lord:  good wishes, praise and prayers.
Shall Suffolk ever have of Margaret. [Going.]

*Farewell, my lord: you will always have*
*my good wishes, praise and prayers.*

SUFFOLK.
Farewell, sweet madam:  but hark you, Margaret;
No princely commendations to my king?

*Farewell, sweet madam: but listen, Margaret;*
*do you have no princely greetings to give my king?*

MARGARET.
Such commendations as becomes a maid,
A virgin and his servant, say to him.

*Give him whatever greetings are suitable for*
*a girl, a virgin and his servant.*

SUFFOLK.
Words sweetly placed and modestly directed.
But, madam, I must trouble you again;
No loving token to his majesty?

*Sweet and modest words.*
*But, madam, I must ask you again;*
*do you have no loving token to give his Majesty?*

MARGARET.
Yes, my good lord, a pure unspotted heart,
Never yet taint with love, I send the king.

*Yes, my good lord, a pure and unstained heart,*
*never yet touched by love, I send that to the King.*

SUFFOLK.
And this withal. *[Kisses her.]*

*And this as well.*

MARGARET.
That for thyself:  I will not so presume
To send such peevish tokens to a king.

*Keep that for yourself: I wouldn't presume*
*to send such worthless tokens to a king.*

*[Exeunt Reignier and Margaret.]*

SUFFOLK. O, wert thou for myself!
But, Suffolk, stay;
Thou mayst not wander in that labyrinth;
There Minotaurs and ugly treasons lurk.
Solicit Henry with her wondrous praise:
Bethink thee on her virtues that surmount,
And natural graces that extinguish art;
Repeat their semblance often on the seas,
That, when thou comest to kneel at Henry's feet,
Thou mayst bereave him of his wits with wonder.

*I wish you were mine!*
*But, stop, Suffolk;*
*you mustn't wander in that labyrinth;*
*there are Minotaurs and ugly treason in there.*
*Tell Henry how wonderful she is:*
*think of her surpassing virtues,*
*and her natural graces that excel all art;*
*keep thinking of them when you are sailing,*
*so that when you come to kneel at Henry's feet,*
*you can astonish him out of his wits.*

*[Exit.]*

# SCENE IV. Camp of the Duke of York in Anjou.

*[Enter York, Warwick, and others.]*

YORK.
Bring forth that sorceress condemn'd to burn.

*Bring out that witch who is condemned to burn.*

*[Enter La Pucelle, guarded, and a Shepherd.]*

SHEPHERD.
Ah, Joan, this kills thy father's heart outright!
Have I sought every country far and near,
And now it is my chance to find thee out,
Must I behold thy timeless cruel death?
Ah, Joan, sweet daughter Joan, I 'll die with thee!

*Ah, Joan, this will kill your father completely!*
*I have looked for you in every place, far and near,*
*and now I have managed to find you,*
*is it only to witness your untimely cruel death?*
*Ah, Joan, sweet daughter Joan, I'll die with you!*

PUCELLE.
Decrepit miser! base ignoble wretch!
I am descended of a gentler blood:
Thou art no father nor no friend of mine.

*You useless low and wretched scum!*
*I come from more noble blood:*
*you are no father and no friend of mine.*

SHEPHERD.
Out, out! My lords, as please you, 'tis not so;
I did beget her, all the parish knows.
Her mother liveth yet, can testify
She was the first fruit of my bachelorship.

*Enough of that! My lords, if you please, this is not true;*
*I fathered her, the whole parish knows it.*
*Her mother is still alive, and can give evidence*
*that she was my first child when I was an apprentice.*

WARWICK.
Graceless! wilt thou deny thy parentage?

*You have no grace! Will you deny your parentage?*

YORK.
This argues what her kind of life hath been,
Wicked and vile; and so her death concludes.

*This shows what kind of life she's led,*
*wicked and horrible; and now her death will end it.*

SHEPHERD.
Fie, Joan, that thou wilt be so obstacle!
God knows thou art a collop of my flesh;
And for thy sake have I shed many a tear:
Deny me not, I prithee, gentle Joan.

*Oh, Joan, why do you have to be so obstinate!*
*God knows that you are made from my flesh;*
*for your sake I have often cried:*
*do not deny me, please, gentle Joan.*

PUCELLE.
Peasant, avaunt! You have suborn'd this man,
Of purpose to obscure my noble birth.

*Peasant, clear off! You have bribed this man,*
*on purpose to hide my noble birth.*

SHEPHERD.
'Tis true, I gave a noble to the priest
The morn that I was wedded to her mother.
Kneel down and take my blessing, good my girl.
Wilt thou not stoop? Now cursed be the time
Of thy nativity! I would the milk
Thy mother gave thee when thou suck'dst her breast,
Had been a little ratsbane for thy sake!
Or else, when thou didst keep my lambs a-field,
I wish some ravenous wolf had eaten thee!
Dost thou deny thy father, cursed drab?

*It's true, I did give a noble to the priest*
*the morning I married her mother.*
*Kneel down and take my blessing, my good girl.*
*Will you not kneel? Now may your birth*
*be cursed! I wish the milk*
*your mother gave you when you suckled at her breast*
*had been rat poison!*
*Or otherwise, when you guarded my lambs in the fields,*
*I wish some hungry wolf had eaten you!*
*Do you deny your father, damned slut?*

O, burn her, burn her! hanging is too good.

*[Exit.]*

YORK.
Take her away; for she hath lived too long,
To fill the world with vicious qualities.

*Take her away; she has lived too long,*
*filling the world with her viciousness.*

PUCELLE.
First, let me tell you whom you have condemn'd:
Not me begotten of a shepherd swain,
But issued from the progeny of kings;
Virtuous and holy; chosen from above,
By inspiration of celestial grace,
To work exceeding miracles on earth.
I never had to do with wicked spirits:
But you, that are polluted with your lusts,
Stain'd with the guiltless blood of innocents,
Corrupt and tainted with a thousand vices,
Because you want the grace that others have,
You judge it straight a thing impossible
To compass wonders but by help of devils.
No, misconceived!  Joan of Arc hath been
A virgin from her tender infancy,
Chaste and immaculate in very thought;
Whose maiden blood, thus rigorously effused,
Will cry for vengeance at the gates of heaven.

*First let me tell you whom you have condemned:*
*I was not born of a shepherd,*
*but came from a line of kings;*
*good and holy; chosen by God,*
*through the inspiration of heaven,*
*to do great miracles on earth.*
*I never associated with wicked spirits:*
*but you, who are polluted with lust,*
*stained with the blood of innocents,*
*corrupted and tainted with a thousand vices,*
*because you are lacking the grace that others have,*
*you think it's completely impossible*
*to work miracles except with the help of devils.*
*No, you don't understand! Joan of Arc has been*
*a virgin since she was born:*
*chaste and immaculate in every thought;*
*if you spill her maiden blood it will*
*cry out for revenge at the gates of heaven.*

YORK.
Aye, aye:  away with her to execution!

*Yes, yes: take her away to be executed!*

WARWICK.
And hark ye, sirs; because she is a maid,
Spare for no faggots, let there be enow:
Place barrels of pitch upon the fatal stake,
That so her torture may be shortened.

*And listen, sirs; because she is a girl,*
*make sure there is a good fire:*
*put barrels of tar on the execution stake,*
*so that her torture can be shortened.*

PUCELLE.
Will nothing turn your unrelenting hearts?
Then, Joan, discover thine infirmity,
That warranteth by law to be thy privilege.
I am with child, ye bloody homicides:
Murder not then the fruit within my womb,
Although ye hale me to a violent death.

*Will nothing change your stony hearts?*
*Then, Joan, tell of your illness,*
*that gives you privileges by law.*
*I am pregnant, you bloody murderers:*
*so don't murder the child in my womb,*
*even though you are dragging me to a violent death.*

YORK.
Now heaven forfend! the holy maid with child!

*Heaven forbid! The holy maid is pregnant!*

WARWICK.
The greatest miracle that e'er ye wrought:
Is all your strict preciseness come to this?

*The greatest miracle that you ever did:*
*has all your good behaviour come to this?*

YORK.
She and the Dauphin have been juggling:
I did imagine what would be her refuge.

*She and the Dauphin have been up to no good:*
*I imagine that this would be her excuse.*

WARWICK.
Well, go to; we'll have no bastards live;
Especially since Charles must father it.

*Well, carry on; we don't want any bastards to survive;*
*especially if Charles is the father of it.*

PUCELLE.
You are deceived; my child is none of his:
It was Alencon that enjoy'd my love.

*You are mistaken; my child is not his:*
*it was Alencon who enjoyed my love.*

YORK.
Alencon! that notorious Machiavel!
It dies, an if it had a thousand lives.

*Alencon! That notorious Machiavelli!*
*We shall kill it, if it had a thousand lives.*

PUCELLE.
O, give me leave, I have deluded you:
'Twas neither Charles nor yet the duke I named,
But Reignier, king of Naples, that prevail'd.

*Oh, excuse me, I lied to you:*
*it wasn't Charles or the Duke I mentioned,*
*but Reignier, King of Naples, who triumphed.*

WARWICK.
A married man! that's most intolerable.

*A married man! We can't have that.*

YORK.
Why, here's a girl!  I think she knows not well
There were so many, whom she may accuse.

*Why, here's a girl! I think she's had so many*
*she doesn't know who to accuse.*

WARWICK.
It's sign she hath been liberal and free.
*affections.*

*It's obvious she has been very generous with her*

YORK.
And yet, forsooth, she is a virgin pure.
Strumpet, thy words condemn thy brat and thee:
Use no entreaty, for it is in vain.

*And yet, by God, she is a pure virgin.*
*Strumpet, your words have condemned your brat and you:*
*do not beg, it is useless.*

PUCELLE.
Then lead me hence; with whom I leave my curse:
May never glorious sun reflex his beams
Upon the country where you make abode:
But darkness and the gloomy shade of death
Environ you, till mischief and despair
Drive you to break your necks or hang yourselves!

*Then take me away; I leave you with this curse:*
*may the glorious sun never shed his light*
*on the country where you live:*
*darkness and the gloomy shade of death*
*will cover you, until trouble and despair*
*cause you to break your neck or hang yourselves!*

*[Exit, guarded.]*

YORK.
Break thou in pieces and consume to ashes,
Thou foul accursed minister of hell!

*May you be broken in pieces and burnt to ashes,*
*you foul cursed agent of hell!*

*[Enter Cardinal Beaufort, Bishop of Winchester, attended.]*

CARDINAL.
Lord regent, I do greet your excellence
With letters of commission from the king.
For know, my lords, the states of Christendom,
Moved with remorse of these outrageous broils,
Have earnestly implored a general peace
Betwixt our nation and the aspiring French;

*Lord Regent, I greet your Excellency*
*bringing my orders from the King.*
*You should know, my lords, that all states in Christendom,*
*deeply regretting these terrible wars,*
*are earnestly begging for peace to be agreed*
*between our nation and the ambitious French;*

And here at hand the Dauphin and his train
Approacheth, to confer about some matter.

YORK.
Is all our travail turn'd to this effect?
After the slaughter of so many peers,
So many captains, gentlemen and soldiers,
That in this quarrel have been overthrown,
And sold their bodies for their country's benefit,
Shall we at last conclude effeminate peace?
Have we not lost most part of all the towns,
By treason, falsehood, and by treachery,
Our great progenitors had conquered?
O, Warwick, Warwick! I foresee with grief
The utter loss of all the realm of France.

WARWICK.
Be patient, York: if we conclude a peace,
It shall be with such strict and severe covenants
As little shall the Frenchmen gain thereby.

[Enter Charles, Alencon, Bastard, Reignier, and others.]

CHARLES.
Since, lords of England, it is thus agreed
That peaceful truce shall be proclaim'd in France,
We come to be informed by yourselves
What the conditions of that league must be.

YORK.
Speak, Winchester; for boiling choler chokes
The hollow passage of my poison'd voice,
By sight of these our baleful enemies.

CARDINAL.
Charles, and the rest, it is enacted thus:
That, in regard King Henry gives consent,
Of mere compassion and of lenity,
To ease your country of distressful war,
And suffer you to breathe in fruitful peace,
You shall become true liegemen to his crown:
And, Charles, upon condition thou wilt swear
To pay him tribute and submit thyself,
Thou shalt be placed as viceroy under him,
And still enjoy the regal dignity.

ALENCON.
Must he be then as shadow of himself?
Adorn his temples with a coronet,
And yet, in substance and authority,
Retain but privilege of a private man?
This proffer is absurd and reasonless.

CHARLES.
'Tis known already that I am possess'd
With more than half the Gallian territories,

and just here are the Dauphin and his followers
coming to speak with you on some matter.

Is this what all our work comes to?
After the slaughter of so many peers,
so many captains, gentlemen and soldiers,
who have lost their lives in this quarrel,
and given their bodies for the benefit of the country,
are we going to meekly agree to a peace?
Haven't we lost most of the towns
our great ancestors conquered
through treason, falsehood and treachery?
Oh, Warwick, Warwick! It's with sorrow
that I predict we shall lose the whole kingdom of France.

Be calm, York: if we agree to a peace,
it will be with such strict and punishing conditions
that it won't do the Frenchmen much good.

Since, lords of England, it has been agreed
that a peaceful truce shall be announced in France,
we have come to be told by you
what the conditions of that agreement must be.

Speak, Winchester; boiling anger chokes
my poisoned throat,
at the sight of these revolting enemies.

Charles, and the rest, this is what has been decreed:
that King Henry has given his consent,
out of simple compassion and kindness,
to take the burden of terrible war from your country
and allow you to prosper in peace,
on condition that you become true servants of his crown:
and Charles, on condition that you will swear
to pay tribute to him and bow down to him,
you shall the given the position of Viceroy under him,
and still enjoy a royal position.

So he has to be a shadow of himself?
You're going to put a crown on his head,
and yet, in every important aspect,
he's just going to be the same as a private citizen?
This offer is absurd and foolish.

You know that I already own
more than half of the territories of France,

And therein reverenced for their lawful king:
Shall I, for lucre of the rest unvanquish'd,
Detract so much from that prerogative,
As to be call'd but viceroy of the whole?
No, lord ambassador, I 'll rather keep
That which I have than, coveting for more,
Be cast from possibility of all.

YORK.
Insulting Charles! hast thou by secret means
Used intercession to obtain a league,
And, now the matter grows to compromise,
Stand'st thou aloof upon comparison?
Either accept the title thou usurp'st,
Of benefit proceeding from our king
And not of any challenge of desert,
Or we will plague thee with incessant wars.

REIGNIER.
My lord, you do not well in obstinacy
To cavil in the course of this contract:
If once it be neglected, ten to one
We shall not find like opportunity.

ALENCON.
To say the truth, it is your policy
To save your subjects from such massacre
And ruthless slaughters as are daily seen,
By our proceeding in hostility;
And therefore take this compact of a truce,
Although you break it when your pleasure serves.

WARWICK.
How say'st thou, Charles? shall our condition stand?

CHARLES.
It shall;
Only reserv'd, you claim no interest
In any of our towns of garrison.

YORK.
Then swear allegiance to his majesty,
As thou art knight, never to disobey
Nor be rebellious to the crown of England
Thou, nor thy nobles, to the crown of England.
So, now dismiss your army when ye please;
Hang up your ensigns, let your drums be still,
For here we entertain a solemn peace.

*[Exeunt.]*

---

*and am revered by them as their lawful King:*
*should I, in return for the half I haven't won,*
*climb down so far from the position I have*
*as to be called viceroy of the whole thing?*
*No, lord ambassador, I would rather keep*
*what I have, not throw away everything*
*to try and get more.*

*Insulting Charles! Have you secretly*
*conspired to form an alliance,*
*and, now we come close to an agreement,*
*claim that your position is equal to ours?*
*Either accept the title you are rejecting,*
*which is offered from the kindness of our king*
*and not because you in any way deserve it,*
*or we will plague you with unending wars.*

*My lord, your obstinacy in refusing*
*the agreement you have been offered is not good:*
*if you reject it, it's ten to one*
*that we'll never be offered such a chance again.*

*To tell the truth, it is your policy*
*to save your subjects from the massacres*
*and ruthless slaughters which are happening daily,*
*as long as we continue with hostilities;*
*and so accept this offer of a truce,*
*even if you are going to break it when you want.*

*What do you say, Charles? Do you agree to our terms?*

*I do;*
*with the reservation that you don't lay any claim*
*to any of our fortified towns.*

*Then swear loyalty to his Majesty,*
*as you are a knight, to never disobey,*
*or be rebellious against, the Crown of England—*
*neither you nor your noblemen.*
*So, disband your army at your convenience;*
*hang up your banners, silence your drums,*
*for here we welcome a solemn peace.*

# SCENE V. London. The royal palace.

*[Enter Suffolk in conference with the King, Gloucester and Exeter.]*

KING.
Your wondrous rare description, noble earl,
Of beauteous Margaret hath astonish'd me.
Her virtues graced with external gifts
Do breed love's settled passions in my heart:
And like as rigor of tempestuous gusts
Provokes the mightiest hulk against the tide,
So am I driven by breath of her renown,
Either to suffer shipwreck or arrive
Where I may have fruition of her love.

*This incredible description, noble Earl,
of the beautiful Margaret has amazed me.
Her goodness combined with external gifts
has created love in my heart:
and as the strength of storm winds
can drive the greatest ship against the tide,
so these words of her virtues make me
determined to risk shipwreck to
win her love.*

SUFFOLK.
Tush, my good lord, this superficial tale
Is but a preface of her worthy praise;
The chief perfections of that lovely dame,
Had I sufficient skill to utter them,
Would make a volume of enticing lines,
Able to ravish any dull conceit:
And, which is more, she is not so divine,
So full-replete with choice of all delights,
But with as humble lowliness of mind
She is content to be at your command;
Command, I mean, of virtuous intents,
To love and honor Henry as her lord.

*Well, my good lord, this quick description
only tells you a little about her goodness;
the real perfections of that lovely woman,
if I had enough skill to describe them,
would fill a volume of enticing lines,
which could wake up even the dullest imagination:
and, what's more, she is not so heavenly,
so packed with so many wonderful virtues,
that she is not content to show a humble
lowness of mind and be at your command;
I mean your right to command her
to love and honour Henry as her lord.*

KING.
And otherwise will Henry ne'er presume.
Therefore, my lord protector, give consent
That Margaret may be England's royal queen.

*Henry will never assume anything different.
So, my lord protector, give your agreement
to Margaret becoming the royal Queen of England.*

GLOUCESTER.
So should I give consent to flatter sin.
You know, my lord, your highness is betroth'd
Unto another lady of esteem:
How shall we then dispense with that contract,
And not deface your honor with reproach?

*If I did I would be agreeing to a sin.
You know, my lord, that your Highness is already
engaged to another great lady:
how shall we break that off
without exposing your honour to criticism?*

SUFFOLK.
As doth a ruler with unlawful oaths;
Or one that, at a triumph having vow'd
To try his strength, forsaketh yet the lists
By reason of his adversary's odds:
A poor earl's daughter is unequal odds,
And therefore may be broke without offense.

*The way a ruler does with unlawful oaths;
or like one who at the jousting has vowed
to test his strength, but refuses to fight
because his opponent is too far below him:
a poor earl's daughter is well below the king,
and so the engagement may be broken without offence.*

GLOUCESTER.
Why, what, I pray, is Margaret more than that?
Her father is no better than an earl,
Although in glorious titles he excel.

*Why, may I ask what makes Margaret higher than that?
Her father is no better than an earl,
however many wonderful titles he has.*

SUFFOLK.

Yes, my lord, her father is a king,
The King of Naples and Jerusalem;
And of such great authority in France,
As his alliance will confirm our peace,
And keep the Frenchmen in allegiance.

GLOUCESTER.
And so the Earl of Armagnac may do,
Because he is near kinsman unto Charles.

EXETER.
Beside, his wealth doth warrant a liberal dower,
Where Reignier sooner will receive than give.

SUFFOLK.
A dower, my lords! disgrace not so your king,
That he should be so abject, base and poor,
To choose for wealth and not for perfect love.
Henry is able to enrich his queen,
And not to seek a queen to make him rich:
So worthless peasants bargain for their wives,
As market-men for oxen, sheep, or horse.
Marriage is a matter of more worth
Than to be dealt in by attorneyship;
Not whom we will; but whom his grace affects,
Must be companion of his nuptial bed:
And therefore, lords, since he affects her most,
It most of all these reasons bindeth us,
In our opinions she should be preferr'd.
For what is wedlock forced but a hell,
An age of discord and continual strife?
Whereas the contrary bringeth bliss,
And is a pattern of celestial peace.
Whom should we match with Henry, being a king,
But Margaret, that is daughter to a king?
Her peerless feature, joined with her birth,
Approves her fit for none but for a king;
Her valiant courage and undaunted spirit,
More than in women commonly is seen,
Will answer our hope in issue of a king;
For Henry, son unto a conqueror,
Is likely to beget more conquerors,
If with a lady of so high resolve
As is fair Margaret he be link'd in love.
Then yield, my lords; and here conclude with me
That Margaret shall be queen, and none but she.

KING.
Whether it be through force of your report,
My noble Lord of Suffolk, or for that
My tender youth was never yet attaint
With any passion of inflaming love,
I cannot tell; but this I am assured,
I feel such sharp dissension in my breast,
Such fierce alarums both of hope and fear,
As I am sick with working of my thoughts.

---

*Yes, my lord, her father is a king,*
*the King of Naples and Jerusalem;*
*he has such great power in France,*
*that an alliance with him will confirm our peace treaty,*
*and keep the Frenchmen loyal.*

*That would be the same with the Earl of Armagnac,*
*because he is closely related to Charles.*

*Besides, his wealth promises a fine dowry,*
*whereas Reignier would rather receive than give.*

*A dowry, my lords? Do not disgrace your king by*
*thinking that he should be so wretched, low and poor*
*as to choose his bride for wealth, and not for perfect love.*
*Henry will make his queen rich,*
*he doesn't need a queen to do that for him;*
*this is how worthless peasants bargain for their wives,*
*like market traders bargaining for cattle, sheep or horses.*
*Marriage is too important to be*
*dealt with by a go-between:*
*it's not whom we want, but whom his grace likes,*
*who must be the one in his marriage bed.*
*And therefore, lords, since he likes her best,*
*that is the decisive factor:*
*we should like her best also.*
*For what is a forced marriage but a hell,*
*an age of arguing and continual strife?*
*Whereas the opposite brings happiness,*
*and is an example of heavenly peace.*
*Whom should we match with Henry, as he is a king,*
*but Margaret, who is daughter to a king?*
*Her matchless looks, combined with her ancestry,*
*show that she this only suitable for a king.*
*Her great courage and undefeated spirit,*
*more than one usually sees in women,*
*will provide us with a such a king as heir that we hope for.*
*For Henry, the son of a conqueror,*
*is likely to father more conquerors,*
*if he marries a lady of such great courage*
*as fair Margaret is.*
*So surrender, my lords, and agree with me*
*that Margaret shall be Queen, nobody but her.*

*Whether it's through the strength of your report,*
*my noble Lord of Suffolk, or that*
*my tender youth has never yet been touched*
*by any passion of burning love,*
*I can't tell; but I know this—*
*I feel such a painful conflict in my heart,*
*such fierce warnings of both hope and fear,*
*that I am sick of thinking about it.*

Take, therefore, shipping; post, my lord, to France;
Agree to any covenants, and procure
That Lady Margaret do vouchsafe to come
To cross the seas to England, and be crown'd
King Henry's faithful and anointed queen:
For your expenses and sufficient charge,
Among the people gather up a tenth.
Be gone, I say; for till you do return,
I rest perplexed with a thousand cares.
And you, good uncle, banish all offense:
If you do censure me by what you were,
Not what you are, I know it will excuse
This sudden execution of my will.
And so, conduct me where, from company,
I may revolve and ruminate my grief.

*[Exit.]*

GLOUCESTER.
Aye, grief, I fear me, both at first and last.

*[Exeunt Gloucester and Exeter.]*

SUFFOLK.
Thus Suffolk hath prevail'd; and thus he goes,
As did the youthful Paris once to Greece,
With hope to find the like event in love,
But prosper better than the Troyan did.
Margaret shall now be queen, and rule the king;
But I will rule both her, the king and realm.

*[Exit.]*

*So take a ship at once, my lord, to France.
Consent to any conditions, and make sure
that the Lady Margaret agrees to come
across the sea to England to be crowned
as King Henry's faithful and anointed Queen.
To make sure you have enough money for expenses,
take a ten percent tax from the people.
Go, I say, for until you return
I shall be tormented by a thousand worries.
And you, good uncle, do not be offended:
if you judge me by what you once were,
not by what you are now, I know you will excuse
my carrying out this decision quickly.
And so take me to a place where, in solitude,
I may meditate upon my suffering.*

*Yes, suffering, I fear, will be the beginning and the end of this.*

*So Suffolk has triumphed; and so he goes,
like the young Paris once went to Greece,
hoping to find the same sort of love,
but have more success than the Trojan did.
Margaret shall now be queen, and rule the king;
but I will rule over her, the king and the country.*

Made in United States
Orlando, FL
12 March 2023

30949134R10057